BIBLE TRIVIA,
JOKES,
AND FUN FACTS
FOR KIDS

Bethany House Books by Troy Schmidt

The 100 Best Bible Verses on Prayer
The 100 Best Bible Verses on Heaven
The 100 Most Encouraging Verses of the Bible

BIBLE TRIVIA, JOKES, AND FUN FACTS FOR KIDS

TROY SCHMIDT

BETHANYHOUSE

a division of Baker Publishing Group
Minneapolis, Minnesota

Published by Bethany House Publishers
11400 Hampshire Avenue South
Bloomington, Minnesota 55438
www.bethanyhouse.com

Bethany House Publishers is a division of
Baker Publishing Group, Grand Rapids, Michigan

Printed in the United States of America

Library of Congress Cataloging-in-Publication Data
Names: Schmidt, Troy, author.
Title: Bible trivia, jokes, and fun facts for kids / Troy Schmidt.
Description: Minneapolis, Minnesota : Bethany House, [2017]
Identifiers: LCCN 2016034662 | ISBN 9780764218460 (trade paper : alk. paper)
Subjects: LCSH: Bible—Miscellanea—Juvenile literature.
Classification: LCC BS539 .S28 2017 | DDC 220—dc23
LC record available at https://lccn.loc.gov/2016034662

Cover design by Dan Pitts

Author represented by Working Title Agency

17 18 19 20 21 22 23   8 7 6 5 4 3 2

HE STANDS at the DOOR and KNOCKS, KNOCKS

Knock, knock
  Who's there?
Noah
  Noah who?
If you don't Noah me, don't open the door!

Knock, knock
  Who's there?
Eve
  Eve who?
It's me, Adam! There's only one other person on the earth. Who do you think it is?!

Knock, knock
  Who's there?
Esau
  Esau who?
Esau me earlier and I said I would stop by.

Knock, knock
　Who's there?
Isaiah
　Isaiah who?
Isaiah again, let me in!

Knock, knock
　Who's there?
Hannah
　Hannah who?
Can you lend me a Hannah and open the door?

Knock, knock
　Who's there?
Israel
　Israel who?
Israel-ly you? I can't wait to see you!

Knock, knock
　Who's there?
Potiphar
　Potiphar who?
I need to borrow a Potiphar rice and beans!

Knock, knock
　Who's there?
Aaron
　Aaron who?
Do you need any shirts to be Aaron-ed?

Knock, knock
   Who's there?
Balaam's donkey
   Balaam's donkey who?
Dude, it's a talking donkey. What more do you need to know?

Knock, knock
   Who's there?
Gideon
   Gideon who?
We have to go to the airport and Gideon a plane.

Knock, knock
   Who's there?
Naomi
   Naomi who?
Naomi $25 and I'm here to collect.

Knock, knock
   Who's there?
Saul
   Saul who?
I Saul you earlier and thought I'd say hi!

Knock, knock
   Who's there?
Goliath
   Goliath who?
Oh, nevermind . . . I'm too tall to fit through this door.

Knock, knock
Who's there?
Solomon
Solomon who?
It's just me—I'm SOLO, MAN.

Knock, knock
Who's there?
Amaziah
Amaziah who?
Yeah, most people don't know me as one of the kings of Judah.

Knock, knock
Who's there?
Methuselah
Methuselah who?
CAN YOU SPEAK UP? I'M 969 YEARS OLD!

Knock, knock
Who's there?
Ezra
Ezra who?
Ezra anyone there who can open this door?

Knock, knock
Who's there?
Nehemiah
Nehemiah who?
I Nehemiah key to get in.

Knock, knock
    Who's there?
ROAR!
    ROAR who?
It's me, Daniel, and I brought a friend!

Knock, knock
    Who's there?
Jonah
    Jonah who?
Do you want to Jonah me and have a whale of a good time?

Knock, knock
    Who's there?
Matthew
    Matthew who?
Gesundheit.

Knock, knock
    Who's there?
Luke
    Luke who?
Luke through the peephole and you'll see it's me.

Knock, knock
    Who's there?
Jesus
    Jesus who?
**If you don't know who I am, then you'd better
    open up the door and let me in!**

CAN'T SiNG IF YOU DON'T KNOW the WORDS Part 1

Fill in the missing word from these psalms to complete the phrase. The right word makes all the difference.

> Heart   Rock   Fingers
> Horses   Light   Tree

A. That person is like a _____ planted by streams of water,
which yields its fruit in season
and whose leaf does not wither—
whatever they do prospers. (Psalm 1:3)

B. When I consider your heavens,
the work of your _____,
the moon and the stars,
which you have set in place,
what is mankind that you are mindful of them,
human beings that you care for them? (Psalm 8:3–4)

C. The Lord is my _____, my fortress and my deliverer;
my God is my rock, in whom I take refuge,
my shield and the horn of my salvation, my stronghold.
(Psalm 18:2)

D. May he give you the desire of your _____
   and make all your plans succeed. (Psalm 20:4)

E. Some trust in chariots and some in _____,
   but we trust in the name of the Lord our God. (Psalm 20:7)

F. The LORD is my _____ and my salvation—
   whom shall I fear?
   The Lord is the stronghold of my life—
   of whom shall I be afraid? (Psalm 27:1)

ARE YOU SMARTER
THAN KiNG SOLOMON?

Which three things did God create on the third day?

- A. Broccoli
- B. Banana
- C. Baboon
- D. Bamboo

Answer: A, B, and D—all of plant life. Land animals were created on the sixth day.

What type of fruit did Adam and Eve eat?

Answer: The Bible never says.

What were the first clothes made out of in the Bible?

Answer: Adam and Eve covered themselves with fig leaves, then God clothed them with animal skins.

Who was the oldest person in the Bible?

Answer: Methuselah, 969 years old. Second was Jared at 962. Adam came in third at only 930 years old. In those days, some would say a 700-year-old person died young!

Which of these was *not* a son of Noah, who took a trip on the ark?

A. Lamech
B. Japheth
C. Shem
D. Ham

Answer: A. Lamech was Noah's father.

Which two animals were specifically mentioned as being on Noah's ark?

A. Dove
B. Eagle
C. Raven
D. Snake
E. Sheep

Answer: A and C. Only the dove and raven were mentioned. The others were definitely on the ark but not mentioned by name.

The shortest name of a city in the Bible is made up of two different vowels. What are those letters?

Answer: A and I. Ai was a city defeated by Joshua.

Which two things did God have Abraham look at to remind him of how many generations he would father?

A. Sheep

B. Sand

C. Stars

D. Sea

Answer: B and C. God wanted Abraham to see that there were so many stars and so many grains of sand and that one day Abraham's descendants would be as numerous.

When Sodom and Gomorrah were destroyed, who did the angels help to get out of the city? (3 answers)

A. Lot

B. Lot's wife

C. Lot's daughters

D. Lot's sons-in-law

E. Lot's mother-in-law

F. Lot's pet donkey

G. The mayor of Sodom

Answer: A, B, and C. Lot's wife got out of the city okay, but she disobeyed by looking back at the city, which is what led to her death.

After Sarah died, Abraham took another wife. What was her name?

A. Rebekah
B. Midian
C. Keturah
D. Jezebel

Answer: C

Which two of these combinations were twins?

A. Jacob/Esau
B. Moses/Aaron
C. Leah/Rachel
D. Isaac/Ishmael
E. Perez/Zerah

Answer: A and E

When Jacob wrestled with an angel, what part of Jacob's body got injured?

A. Twisted arm
B. Broken toe
C. Poked in the eye
D. Popped in the hip

Answer: D. The angel twisted and popped Jacob's hip socket, causing him to limp.

Which of these people had their name changed in the Bible?
(4 answers)

    A. Peter

    B. Jacob

    C. Abraham

    D. Moses

    E. Paul

    F. David

Answer: A, B, C, and E. Peter's original name was Simon, Jacob became Israel, Abraham started out as Abram, and Paul originally was called Saul.

Which of these two men (who were known by their occupations) were in prison with Joseph?

    A. The hairdresser

    B. The cupbearer

    C. The candlestick maker

    D. The chief baker

    E. The homemaker

Answer: B and D

Whose bones made the trip with Moses from Egypt to Israel?

Answer: Joseph. It was a request he made before he died. The Israelites had to carry those bones themselves since FedEx was not up and running in those days.

What does the name *Moses* mean?

    A. Man with long beard

    B. Guy who saw God

    C. Someone drawn from the water

    D. Sea-parter

Answer: C. Pharaoh's daughter named him Moses when she pulled him out of the Nile.

In order to impress Pharaoh, Moses had a staff turn into what?

    A. A snake

    B. An arrow

    C. A loaf of bread

    D. A giant pencil

Answer: A. But when the magicians did the same trick, Moses' snake ate their snakes. Top that, magicians!

What does the word *manna* mean?

    A. Mmmm, delicious

    B. What is that?

    C. Tastes sweet

    D. Can I have more?

Answer: B. The Israelites were surprised by the substance that could be made into bread. They obviously had never encountered bread appearing out of thin air before.

Which three items were in the ark of the covenant and carried around by the Israelites during their 40 years in the wilderness?

A. Aaron's rod

B. A jar of manna

C. A rock of ages

D. The stone tablets

E. A jar of water from the Red Sea

F. Quail under glass

Answer: A, B, and D. They all represented significant moments in God's rescue of the people from Egypt.

Which three of these things were on the "do not" list for a Nazirite?

A. Don't cut your hair.

B. Don't eat honey.

C. Don't eat grapes.

D. Don't touch dead things.

Answer: A, C, and D. The commands reminded the Nazirites of their vow to God to stay pure.

What did Moses hit with his staff that caused water to gush out for the Israelites in the wilderness?

Answer: A rock

How many Israelite spies slipped into the Promised Land to check it out?

Answer: Twelve, one for each tribe. While 10 were scared of the big giants they saw there, only two showed faith that God would help them (Joshua and Caleb).

What two books of the Bible list the 10 Commandments in order?

A. Matthew
B. Deuteronomy
C. Proverbs
D. Exodus

Answer: B and D

Which four of these people were part of Moses' family?

A. Jethro
B. Joshua
C. Miriam
D. Aaron
E. Caleb
F. Zipporah

Answers: A, Jethro, his father-in-law; C, Miriam, his sister; D, Aaron, his brother; F, Zipporah, his wife.

Which four things did God tell the Israelites to do to make the walls of Jericho fall?

A. March around the city once a day for six days

B. March around seven times on the seventh day

C. Sing songs over and over again, driving the people crazy inside the city

D. Boo and hiss as they marched around the city

E. Blow the trumpets loudly

F. Bang the drums slowly

G. Carry the ark of the covenant at the front of the procession

Answers: A, B, E, and G. God said if they followed His commands precisely they would have success. And they did.

Which of these feats of strength did Samson do? (5 answers)

A. Tie torches to foxtails

B. Run faster than a speeding bullet

C. Kill an army with a donkey's jawbone

D. Tear out a city's gate

E. Tear down a building by pushing on the pillars

F. Move a mountain

G. Kill a lion with his bare hands

Answers: A, C, D, E, and G. Samson was the Superman of his day.

What did Gideon lay outside one night that was wet with dew in the morning, and then lay out the next night but was dry as a bone the following morning?

Answer: A sheep's fleece. Gideon asked for the fleece to be wet and the ground dry and vice versa in order to confirm that it was God asking him to fight the enemy.

When Gideon attacked the Midianites, what three objects did his army use to confuse and defeat the enemy?

A. Scarecrows

B. Trumpets

C. Jars

D. Bread sticks

E. Snowballs

F. Torches

Answer: B, C, and F. His army put torches inside jars. Then when they were inside the camps, the soldiers blew the trumpets and busted the jars. The sudden light and sound confused the enemies, who started attacking themselves.

What physical characteristic of Saul made him a popular choice to be king among the people in 1 Samuel?

A. He was tall, a head above everyone else

B. He had six-pack abs

C. He had nice hair

D. He could whistle

Answer: A

What two animals did David brag about killing when he was a shepherd?

A. Wolves

B. Lions

C. Bears

D. Snakes

Answers: B and C. But David said to Saul, "Your servant has been keeping his father's sheep. When a lion or a bear came and carried off a sheep from the flock, I went after it, struck it and rescued the sheep from its mouth" (1 Samuel 17:34–35).

How many stones did David use to kill Goliath?

Answer: Only one, though he picked up five.

Which three of these were a reward King Saul promised someone if they killed Goliath?

A. Great riches

B. No taxes

C. A big trophy

D. His daughter's hand in marriage

Answer: A, B, and D. No trophies were handed out in those days.

What was the name of the valley where David killed Goliath?

A. Valley of the Shadow of Death

B. Valley of Elah

C. Death Valley

D. San Fernando Valley

Answer: B. Located west of Bethlehem.

God told King Solomon to ask Him for whatever he wanted. What did King Solomon ask God for?

A. Long life

B. Wealth

C. Honor

D. Wisdom

E. Unlimited cookies

Answer: D. Solomon asked only for wisdom, but God also threw in wealth and honor.

It took Solomon seven years to build the temple. How long did it take to build his palace?

Answer: Fourteen years. Something wrong with this picture?

King Solomon had incredible wisdom. Which of these subjects did the Bible say he had great insight into? (5 answers)

- A. Plants
- B. Sports
- C. Animals
- D. Fish
- E. Reptiles
- F. Weather
- G. Birds
- H. Fractions and math

Answer: A, C, D, E, and G. Solomon definitely would have aced any biology quiz.

The Bible says Solomon wrote 3,000 proverbs and 1,000 what?

- A. Jokes
- B. Recipes
- C. Novels
- D. Songs

Answer: D. There's a book in the Bible called the Song of Solomon. Two psalms, 72 and 127, are also attributed to Solomon.

On what mountain did Elijah square off against the 450 prophets of Baal?

- A. Mount Carmel
- B. Mount Everest
- C. Mount Sinai
- D. Space Mountain

Answer: A

Which of these books are attributed to King Solomon as the author? (3 answers)

    A. Ecclesiastes

    B. Job

    C. Song of Songs

    D. Proverbs

    E. Isaiah

    F. Ezra

Answer: A, C, and D

Joash was the youngest king in the Bible. What was his age?

    A. 7 years old

    B. 18 years old

    C. 38 years old

    D. 88 years old

Answer: A. His first rule was to bring recess back to school. J/k.

Which four of these people were "friends" of Job and gave him advice during his trials?

    A. Haggai

    B. Tobiah

    C. Zophar

    D. Bildad

    E. Eliphaz

    F. Elihu

    G. Bob

Answer: C, D, E, and F. God later considered their advice meaningless and scolded them.

Job had a tough time in the Bible. Which of these terrible things happened to him?

A. His oxen, camels, and donkeys were stolen
B. His brother's house collapsed in a windstorm
C. He got painful sores
D. His sheep burned up
E. His servants were killed

Answer: All of them happened to Job. Yes, even his sheep burned up when fire fell from the sky. It was Job's "terrible, horrible, no good, very bad day."

Which of these two-letter names are actually places in the Bible? (4 answers)

A. OZ
B. AI
C. UZ
D. MO
E. UR
F. OK
G. AR

Answer: B, C, E, and G. Ai was a city Joshua conquered, Job was from Uz, Abraham lived in Ur, and Ar was a nation in Numbers 21:15.

Which three places did Jonah visit on his travels?

    A. Joppa

    B. Egypt

    C. Jericho

    D. Nineveh

    E. Tarshish

    F. Disney World

Answer: A, D, and E. After God called Jonah, he traveled to Tarshish, where he caught a boat at Joppa, but God redirected him to Nineveh.

In the Song of Songs, the writer compared a woman's hair to a flock of what?

Answer: Goats. Isn't that romantic?

In the Song of Songs, the writer compared a woman's teeth to a flock of what?

Answer: Sheep who had just been sheared, apparently meaning they were really white, which is a big deal—especially before the invention of toothpaste.

OLD TESTAMENT SCRAMBLE

Unscramble these letters to find books in the Old Testament.

1. I CUT EVILS

2. MONEY OR DUET

3. SEE SIGN

4. OX DUES

5. BURNS ME

6. HURT

7. RAZE

8. I AM HE HEN

9. HE REST

10. SEE CAT SLICES

11. SONS OF GONGS

12. I JEER HAM

13. MAN ATE TONSIL

14. NAILED

15. A SHOE

16. I HAD BOA

17. HUMAN

18. HAZE CHAIR

WHO ART THOU?

Find a friend and read these clues one at a time without reading ahead. By which clue can your friend guess who or what is being described? The sooner they guess, the more points they receive. Remember, they only get one guess.

100 Points: I hang out in gardens.
75 Points: Especially near fruit trees.
50 Points: Don't trust me.
25 Points: God cursed me to the ground.
10 Points: I tempted Eve.

The snake (aka Satan)

100 Points: I have three sons.
75 Points: I like to build.
50 Points: I became a zoologist.
25 Points: I never knew how to sail.
10 Points: I was the captain of an ark.

Noah

100 Points: I'm a mother.

75 Points: I laughed.

50 Points: I traveled long distances with my husband.

25 Points: I was a mother at a very old age.

10 Points: My husband is Abraham.

Sarah

100 Points: I'm red.

75 Points: I'm hairy.

50 Points: I struggled with my brother.

25 Points: I love archery and delicious stew.

10 Points: My brother was Isaac.

Esau

100 Points: They call me a dreamer.

75 Points: I wore fancy, colorful clothes.

50 Points: I had many brothers.

25 Points: I became as powerful as a pharaoh.

10 Points: My dad was Jacob.

Joseph

100 Points: I talk to fires.

75 Points: I walk through water.

50 Points: I eat amazing bread.

25 Points: You can find me on mountains.

10 Points: Let my people go.

Moses

100 Points: I hate haircuts.

75 Points: I like to light foxes on fire.

50 Points: Nag me and I'll tell you my secrets.

25 Points: Blind me and I'll knock down your city.

10 Points: I was the strongest man in the Bible.

Samson

100 Points: Hi, I'm from Gath.

75 Points: My forehead is an easy target.

50 Points: It's true: The taller they are, the harder they fall.

25 Points: I'm a big bully.

10 Points: Really, a shepherd took me down?

Goliath

100 Points: I lived in the land of Uz, not Oz.

75 Points: God and Satan talk about me.

50 Points: I had the worst day in the Bible.

25 Points: The sores on my body were so bad I scraped them with pottery.

10 Points: My friends gave me bad advice.

Job

100 Points: I was the king when the ark first arrived at the temple.

75 Points: I helped to build the temple.

50 Points: I asked for wisdom and I got it.

25 Points: I wrote 3,000 proverbs.

10 Points: I got the job because my dad was King David.

Solomon

100 Points: I'm no Jewish princess. I'm a queen.

75 Points: I like to prepare banquets.

50 Points: My uncle Mordecai is my closest advisor.

25 Points: I won a beauty contest to become queen.

10 Points: Because of my faith, I saved many Jews from dying.

Esther

100 Points: Don't tell me not to pray.

75 Points: I was the advisor to many kings.

50 Points: I sometimes go on a vegetarian diet.

25 Points: My best friends are hot . . . literally.

10 Points: Some of my other friends are lions.

Daniel

100 Points: I'm a runner.

75 Points: I don't like my enemies at all.

50 Points: I'm a swimmer and I like to jump overboard, especially during storms.

25 Points: I might smell like fish vomit.

10 Points: I give fish a stomachache.

Jonah

100 Points: I used to hang out with sheep all the time.

75 Points: Then I started hanging out with soldiers.

50 Points: I took out this big dude with a sling and a rock.

25 Points: Then I became a king and a songwriter.

10 Points: My son and his son and his son and his son . . . all became kings.

David

10-4-10

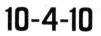

List these 10 plagues that struck Egypt during the time of Moses in the order they happened in the Bible.

____ Darkness

____ Frogs

____ Nile turned to blood

____ Plague on the firstborn

____ Plague on livestock

____ Hail

____ Flies

____ Gnats

____ Locusts

____ Boils

WORDS in a WORD FROM the WORD

OLD TESTAMENT

How many words can you make from the following words found in the Word?

ABRAHAM—We found 8 possible words. Can you find more?

_____   _____   _____

_____   _____   _____

_____   _____

MOSES—We found 6 possible words. Can you find more?

_____   _____   _____

_____   _____   _____

EGYPT—We found 5 possible words. Can you find more?

_____   _____   _____

_____   _____

AARON—We found 7 possible words. Can you find more?

_____   _____   _____

_____   _____   _____

_____

JOSEPH—We found 17 possible words. Can you find more?

_____   _____   _____

_____   _____   _____

_____   _____   _____

_____   _____   _____

_____   _____   _____

_____   _____

TEMPLE—We found 11 possible words. Can you find more?

_____   _____   _____

_____   _____   _____

_____   _____   _____

_____   _____

JOSHUA—We found 6 possible words. Can you find more?

_____   _____   _____

_____   _____   _____

ELIJAH—We found 7 possible words. Can you find more?

_____   _____   _____

_____   _____   _____

_____

JERICHO—We found 15 possible words. Can you find more?

_____   _____   _____

_____   _____   _____

_____   _____   _____

_____   _____   _____

_____   _____   _____

SAMSON—We found 14 possible words. Can you find more?

_____   _____   _____

_____   _____   _____

_____   _____   _____

_____   _____   _____

_____   _____

GIDEON—We found 20 possible words. Can you find more?

_____   _____   _____

_____   _____   _____

_____   _____   _____

_____   _____   _____

_____   _____   _____

_____   _____   _____

_____   _____

DAVID—We found 9 possible words. Can you find more?

_____   _____   _____

_____   _____   _____

_____   _____   _____

SOLOMON—We found 15 possible words. Can you find more?

_____   _____   _____

_____   _____   _____

_____   _____   _____

_____   _____   _____

_____   _____   _____

GOLIATH—We found 24 possible words. Can you find more?

_____   _____   _____

_____   _____   _____

_____   _____   _____

_____   _____   _____

_____   _____   _____

_____   _____   _____

_____   _____   _____

_____   _____   _____

DANIEL—We found 21 possible words. Can you find more?

_____   _____   _____

_____   _____   _____

_____   _____   _____

_____   _____   _____

_____   _____   _____

_____   _____   _____

_____   _____   _____

RAINBOW—We found 34 possible words. Can you find more?

_____   _____   _____

_____   _____   _____

_____   _____   _____

_____   _____   _____

_____   _____   _____

_____   _____   _____

_____   _____   _____

_____   _____   _____

_____   _____   _____

_____   _____   _____

_____

BiBLE BANTER

How do we know God loves baseball?

Because when He created the world, He did it in the big-inning.

Why does God love mangos and math?

Because He's always telling us to be fruitful and multiply.

What do Creation and Paul Revere have in common?

First came land, then the sea.

When did God teach first aid in Genesis?

When He gave Adam mouth-to-mouth resuscitation.

What kind of cheese did God make on the seventh day?

Swiss, because it is hole-y.

Why did Adam get hungry when God made woman?

Because he heard God was making something out of ribs.

Which book of the Bible is your dogs' favorite?

Rooooooth!

What kind of colorful weapon did Noah use?

A rain-bow.

Was Abraham an uncle to many nephews?

No, but he was an uncle to a Lot.

Because of his deception in the Garden, what did the snake change forever?

HISSSS-tory

Why was Smokey Bear angry at Moses?

Because Moses was burning bushes out in the wilderness.

Why do cows and bees love the Promised Land?

Because they heard it was the land of milk and honey.

Why was the ruler of Egypt mad at the Israelites?

Because they wanted to move so Pharaoh-way!

Why did Moses have such a hard time as a baby?

Because he was in de-Nile.

Why did the Israelites trade desserts with each other?
Because God said a pie-for-a-pie.

What do the Israelites and a bad quarterback have in common?
They both throw a Passover.

Why did Moses count the Israelites two times in the Bible?
Because he wanted to make sure they came to their census.

Why did Moses keep sneezing every time he went up the mountain?
Because he came down with a Sinai infection.

Which book of the Bible can you always count on?
Numbers.

What city was a building contractor's nightmare?
Jericho, because the walls all fell down.

What did Samson say to his barber?
Nothing, they never saw each other.

What kind of music did David like?
Rock 'n' roll. He liked to throw a rock and watch Goliath's head roll to the ground.

Why was it important that David was a shepherd before he was king?

Because he knew the good from the baaaaaaaad.

How do we know Goliath went insane?

Because after fighting David, he lost his head.

What did Absalom say when he died?

"Hair today; gone tomorrow."

Which NFL football team fed the prophet Elijah when he needed food?

The Ravens

Which NFL team did Daniel tame in the final minutes of the match?

The Lions

Which NFL team never invited David to a game?

The Giants

Which NFL team got nervous every Passover?

The Rams

Why did Elijah enjoy playing Candyland?

Because he loved to play games on Mount Carmel.

Who was voted Miss Persia 478 BC?

Esther, who won a beauty contest and got the king's hand in marriage.

What three guys were the best bakers in the Bible?

Shadrach, Meshach, and Abednego, because they spent a lot of time in the oven.

Why was Daniel so hard to trust?

Because of his lyin' (lion).

Why was Jeremiah known as the weeping prophet?

Because he was sad . . . duh!

Who was the most suspicious prophet in the Bible?

Jonah, because when he was around, something always smelled fishy.

What kind of music was playing at the Resurrection?

ROCK and ROLL.

Why is the Bible so concerned about what kind of pants people wore throughout the ages?

Because it's always talking about the Levis and jean-ealogy.

Who was the first Scrooge in the Bible?

King Herod, because he rejected the first Christmas.

Where did the wise men shop for the baby Jesus?

Bed, Bethlehem, and Beyond

Why do some think the shepherds saw celebrities on the night of Jesus' birth?

Because they were star struck.

How do we know John the Baptist liked the Chicago Bulls?

Because he regularly went to the (Michael) Jordan River.

How do we know Jesus never made it as a baker?

Because He kept telling people that man does not live on bread alone.

Why was Jesus always fighting with the Pharisees?

Because He didn't like their be-attitudes.

Why does the Bible call going without food a "fast"?

Because when it's over, that's how quickly you run to the refrigerator.

Why does God love bald people?

Because the Bible says God has the hairs of our heads numbered, so bald people make His job easier.

Why were pigs the best-dressed animals in the Bible?

Because apparently people kept throwing their pearls at them. (Matthew 7:6)

Which of Jesus' apostles was a professional wrestler?

Peter, because Jesus called him The Rock.

Who did Jesus warn us about at Halloween?

Pharisees, because they dress up like wolves in sheep's clothing.

How do we know Jesus was good at math?

Because He multiplied bread and fish, and He talked about a house divided against itself.

Why wasn't Jesus very good at sewing?

Because he thought it was easier to put a camel through the eye of a needle.

Why was Jesus' appearance at the temple a significant moment?

Because that's when the tables turned.

What did Jesus say to the devil when he tried to get ahead of Him in line?

Get behind me, Satan!

What did Elizabeth's baby do inside her when she met Mary pregnant with Jesus?

Jumping Johns.

Why do we know Joseph and Mary weren't crazy going to Bethlehem?

Because they came to their census.

How do we know Jesus never took the SAT?

Because He said, "Do not put the Lord your God to the test!"

What was Peter's last name?

Peter Fisherman

When Jesus healed the paralyzed man, how do we know a party broke out?

Because the paralyzed man's friends raised the roof!

What kind of stories did Jesus tell about fruit?
Pear-ables

Why didn't Jesus like the religious leaders of His day?
Because they weren't fair-you-see.

Why did Jesus tell corn pickers to listen closely?
Because He kept saying, "Whoever has ears, let them hear."

Where did the Prodigal Son eventually get a job at the mall?
At the once-lost-but-now-found department.

Why did Jesus tell dogs they couldn't have more than one owner?
Because He said no one can serve two masters.

How long did Jesus spend with Zacchaeus in Jericho?
Just a short time.

Why would Jesus make a good dentist?
Because He knows the tooth and how to set it free.

What day of the week did Jesus slap high fives?
Palm Sunday

How do we know the apostles ate hot sauce during Pentecost?

Because it said they suddenly were overcome with tongues of fire.

When traveling down the road to Damascus, Paul had a collision with God. What happened?

Paul was blindsided.

How do you know that you are filled with the fruits of the Spirit?

You're bananas for God and you're berry glad He saved you.

How do we know money doesn't grow on a tree?

Because the Bible says money is the root of all kinds of evil.

How do we know the Word of God is sharper than any two-edged sword?

Because it cuts through all the bologna in life.

10-4-10

In what order do these 10 Commandments appear in Exodus 20? Number them 1 to 10.

____ You shall not make a false idol.

____ Honor your mother and father.

____ Do not commit adultery.

____ Do not covet your neighbor's things.

____ Do not misuse God's name.

____ Do not give a false testimony about your neighbor.

____ Do not steal.

____ Remember the Sabbath day and make it holy.

____ Do not murder.

____ You shall have no other gods before God.

CAN'T SING IF YOU DON'T KNOW the WORDS Part 2

Fill in the missing word from these psalms to complete the phrase. The right word makes all the difference.

> Deer   House   Gates
> Courts   Years   Heart

A. One thing I ask from the Lord,
     this only do I seek:
   that I may dwell in the _____ of the Lord
     all the days of my life,
   to gaze on the beauty of the Lord
     and to seek him in his temple. (Psalm 27:4)

B. As the _____ pants for streams of water,
     so my soul pants for you, my God. (Psalm 42:1)

C. Create in me a pure _____, O God,
     and renew a steadfast spirit within me.
   Do not cast me from your presence
     or take your Holy Spirit from me.
   Restore to me the joy of your salvation
     and grant me a willing spirit, to sustain me. (Psalm 51:10–12)

D. Better is one day in your _____
    than a thousand elsewhere;
  I would rather be a doorkeeper in the house of my God
    than dwell in the tents of the wicked. (Psalm 84:10)

E. A thousand _____ in your sight
    are like a day that has just gone by,
    or like a watch in the night. (Psalm 90:4)

F. Enter his _____ with thanksgiving
    and his courts with praise;
    give thanks to him and praise his name. (Psalm 100:4)

MATCHES MADE in HEAVEN

The Perfect Match

Match the man on the left with his wife on the right.

Adam	Hannah
Abraham	Sapphira
Isaac	Zipporah
Moses	Eve
Elkanah	Esther
King Xerxes	Sarah
Ananias	Rebekah

Answers: Adam/Eve, Abraham/Sarah, Isaac/Rebekah, Moses/Zipporah, Elkanah/Hannah, King Xerxes/Esther, Ananias/Sapphira

Like Father, Like Son

Match the man on the left with his son on the right.

Adam   Rehoboam

Noah   Ishmael

Abraham   Absalom

Isaac   Seth

Jacob   Obed

Moses   Gershom

Boaz   Ham

David   Levi

Solomon   Esau

O Brother, Where Are You?

Match the person on the left with his brother on the right.

Cain   Abinadab

Jacob   Reuben

Joseph   Abel

Moses   James

David   Andrew

Peter   Esau

John   Aaron

The Name Game

When Daniel was taken to Babylon, the Babylonians changed his name to Belteshazzar. Match his friends' original Jewish names on the left with their Babylonian names on the right.

Mishael   Shadrach

Azariah   Meshach

Hananiah   Abednego

Dream Matcher

Match the person on the left with the thing they saw in their dream on the right.

Jacob	Angel saying "Don't divorce"
Joseph (son of Jacob)	Seven skinny cows
Joseph (father of Jesus)	Sun, moon, 11 stars
Pilate's wife	Statue made of four materials
Pharaoh	Stairway to heaven
Nebuchadnezzar	Jesus was innocent

Answers:

Jacob/Stairway to heaven. Jacob saw a stairway (some interpretations say "ladder") that led from earth to heaven and was traveled by scores of angels. This occurred at Bethel and revealed God's activity in the region.

Joseph (son of Jacob)/Sun, moon, 11 stars—Joseph's dream showed the sun, moon, and 11 stars bowing down to him. This dream meant that one day his whole family would bow down to him. It came true when his family traveled to Egypt and encountered him as the second in command under Pharaoh.

Joseph (father of Jesus)/Angel saying "Don't divorce." Joseph thought about leaving Mary when he heard she was pregnant, but the angel in his dream told him not to.

Pilate's wife/Jesus was innocent. Pilate's wife had a dream that caused her to suffer all night. She felt the dream was telling her that Jesus was innocent.

Pharaoh/Seven skinny cows. Pharaoh's dream set off the need to find someone to interpret what he experienced. Joseph understood that the seven skinny cows meant seven years of famine for Egypt.

Nebuchadnezzar/Statue made of four materials. The King of Babylon saw this four-tiered statue, and Daniel interpreted the dream to warn the king that there were four major world powers coming in history: the Babylonians, the Persians, the Greeks, and the soon-coming Romans.

DiD YOU KNOW? Part 1

Old Testament

DID YOU KNOW that the first musician of the Bible was Jubal? It says he played stringed instruments and pipes. A regular one-man band. (Genesis 4:21)

DID YOU KNOW that Noah's ark was longer than a football field? The Bible says the ark was 300 cubits long, 50 cubits wide, and 30 cubits high. **What's a cubit?** A cubit is about 18 inches, the average length from an adult fingertip to the elbow. (There were no tape measures in those days.) That means Noah's ark was 5,400 inches / 450 feet / 150 yards long. It was 900 inches / 75 feet / 25 yards wide. It was 540 inches / 45 feet / 15 yards high.

An American football field is 100 yards long—120 if you add in the end zones—and 53 yards wide. So Noah's ark was 30 yards *longer* than a football field from the end of each end zone, but half as wide.

Since it was three decks high on the inside, that means each floor was 13 feet high. A fully grown giraffe stands 16 feet high, so either baby giraffes were on the ark or the adult giraffe had neck problems when he got off. (Genesis 6)

DID YOU KNOW Mount Ararat, where Noah's ark landed and finally rested, can still be found in Turkey today? Mount Ararat is on the eastern side of Turkey, bordering Iran and Armenia. It is actually made up of two side-by-side mountains: Greater Ararat and Lesser Ararat. Greater Ararat is 16,854 feet high and Lesser Ararat is 12,782. Mount Ararat is an inactive volcano and snow-capped year-round. But don't go and try to find Noah's ark—it's not there. (Genesis 8:4)

DID YOU KNOW the mountain that Abraham took his son Isaac to and offered to sacrifice him on (but was stopped by God) is the same mountain Jesus offered himself as a sacrifice on the cross (but was not stopped by God)?

The mountain was Mount Moriah, mentioned in Genesis.

Then God said, "Take your son, your only son, whom you love—Isaac—and go to the region of Moriah. Sacrifice him there as a burnt offering on a mountain I will show you" (Genesis 22:2).

Then later, when King Solomon built the temple in Jerusalem, he did it on the same mountain.

Then Solomon began to build the temple of the Lord in Jerusalem on Mount Moriah, where the Lord had appeared to his father David. It was on the threshing floor of Araunah the Jebusite, the place provided by David. (2 Chronicles 3:1)

While God stopped Abraham from sacrificing Isaac, He did not stop His own son from dying by the hands of the Romans. God wanted to see if Abraham had faith to trust Him. He also wanted people to see that a couple thousand years later, He knew that Jesus would come to die for our sins.

DID YOU KNOW the prophet Elisha was bald? When a group of teenagers made fun of his lack of hair, God had bears come out of the woods and attack them. So don't make fun of your dad or your Uncle Eli for being bald—unless you are ready to fight off some hungry bears. (2 Kings 2:23)

DID YOU KNOW that the Dead Sea is the lowest point on Earth? It's 1,407 feet below sea level. And the Dead Sea itself is 997 feet deep. The sea is dead because of its high concentration of salt (or saline). Because of the super-salty water, no animals can live in it.

Why is the Dead Sea dead, you ask? Being the lowest point on Earth, water runs in but can't run out. So all of the unhealthy chemicals that wash in from all over Israel can't go anywhere.

Some people believe that the destruction of Sodom and Gomorrah (Genesis 19) aided in the "death" of the Dead Sea. The Bible says that burning sulphur (a type of salt) fell from the sky and destroyed the towns; archaeologists think Sodom and Gomorrah were either right on the sea or very close by.

DID YOU KNOW Moses was 80 years old when he asked Pharaoh to let the Israelites go? Moses grew up in Egypt under the care of Pharaoh's daughter until the age of 40. Then he spent another 40 years in the desert until God spoke to him through the burning bush. (Stephen talked about Moses' age in Acts 7.) Moses then led the Israelites through the wilderness for another 40 years, dying at the age of 120. Who has time for retirement?

DID YOU KNOW Jesus quoted the Old Testament books Exodus, Deuteronomy, Psalms, and Isaiah more than any other Old Testament book? Jesus quoted Deuteronomy three times when confronting the devil's temptation (Deuteronomy 6:16, 8:3, 6:13) and when discussing the greatest commandments (Deuteronomy 6:4–5). He quoted Exodus when discussing the Law, and Psalms when confronting the Pharisees. Jesus focused on Isaiah when talking about His fulfillment of Isaiah's prophecies. Maybe you should read up on those books, too, since Jesus knew them so well!

DID YOU KNOW how many chapters, verses, and words are in the Bible?*

	Chapters	Verses	Words
Old Testament	929	23,214	622,771
New Testament	260	7,959	184,590
Bible	1,189	31,173	807,361

DID YOU KNOW that when Jesus said the famous phrase from the cross, "My God, my God, why have you forsaken me?" He was quoting the first verse of Psalm 22? But He was also pointing out to those around Him that the prophecies in that psalm were happening to Him at that moment.

The Prophecy in Psalm 22 . . .

> But I am a worm and not a man,
>> scorned by everyone, despised by the people.
> All who see me mock me;
>> they hurl insults, shaking their heads.
> "He trusts in the Lord," they say,
>> "let the Lord rescue him.
> Let him deliver him,
>> since he delights in him."

Psalm 22:6–8

. . . Came True at the Cross

The people stood watching, and the rulers even sneered at him. They said, "He saved others; let him save himself if he is God's Messiah, the Chosen One."

Luke 23:35

* *NASB Open Bible* (Nashville: Thomas Nelson, 1977), 1227, http://www.never thirsty.org/pp/corner/read2/r00722.html.

The Prophecy in Psalm 22 . . .

> My mouth is dried up like a potsherd,
>   and my tongue sticks to the roof of my mouth;
>   you lay me in the dust of death.
>
> Psalm 22:15

. . . Came True at the Cross

Immediately one of them ran and got a sponge. He filled it with wine vinegar, put it on a staff, and offered it to Jesus to drink.

Matthew 27:48

The Prophecy in Psalm 22 . . .

> Dogs surround me,
>   a pack of villains encircles me;
>   they pierce my hands and my feet.
>
> Psalm 22:16

. . . Came True at the Cross

(Later when Jesus appeared to the disciples after the crucifixion) So the other disciples told him, "We have seen the Lord!" But he said to them, "Unless I see the nail marks in his hands and put my finger where the nails were, and put my hand into his side, I will not believe."

John 20:25

The Prophecy in Psalm 22 . . .

> All my bones are on display;
>   people stare and gloat over me.
> They divide my clothes among them
>   and cast lots for my garment.
>
> Psalm 22:17–18

... Came True at the Cross

When they had crucified him, they divided up his clothes by casting lots.

Matthew 27:35

The Prophecy in Psalm 22 ...

> Posterity will serve him;
> > future generations will be told about the Lord.
> They will proclaim his righteousness,
> > declaring to a people yet unborn:
> > He has done it!

Psalm 22:30–31

... Came True at the Cross

And when the centurion, who stood there in front of Jesus, saw how he died, he said, "Surely this man was the Son of God!"

Mark 15:39

Jesus pointed out how much of the Old Testament was coming true right before the people's eyes in just the one chapter of Psalms!

DID YOU KNOW there is only one Old Testament book that is one chapter in length (Obadiah), and four New Testament books that are only one chapter in length (Philemon, 2 John, 3 John, Jude)? There is also only one book in the whole Bible that is two chapters long: Haggai. Eight books are three chapters long.

DID YOU KNOW Goliath was between 9 and 10 feet tall? Most texts say he was "six cubits and a span" (1 Samuel 17:4). While a *cubit* is approximately 18 inches—the distance from your elbow to the end of your finger—a *span* is about the width of your hand—from pinky to thumb spread out (about 9 inches, or a half cubit). So 6 (cubits) x 18 inches + 9 inches (1 span) = 117 inches (9 feet and 9 inches).

Could a man stand 9 feet tall? The tallest man in recorded history was Robert Wadlow, at 8 feet 11 inches, and he was very frail in health, dying at the age of 22 (hardly a warrior).

However, other Bible texts (the Dead Sea Scrolls text of Samuel, the first-century historian Josephus, and the fourth-century Septuagint manuscripts) give Goliath a different height—4 cubits and a span, which comes out to 6 feet 9 inches. That's just a little taller than Lebron James and shorter than Shaq, both of whom are warriors on the basketball court!

God can make any person to be any height, and in that day when people were shorter (probably averaging around five feet), Goliath would have been a bigger giant (even by our standards today)!

DID YOU KNOW that when Solomon had the temple built, they tried to do it quietly? The gigantic rocks for the temple were pulled out from a quarry far away and prepared at that location, so when they arrived, no hammering and chiseling needed to occur.

> In building the temple, only blocks dressed at the quarry were used, and no hammer, chisel or any other iron tool was heard at the temple site while it was being built.
>
> 1 Kings 6:7

Why did they do this? First of all, the noise would be unbearable and nonstop. The residents of Jerusalem (and King Solomon) wanted a little peace and quiet. Also, it created a mood of reverence and reflection at the temple. While noises needed to occur—it took seven years to build—they did everything they could to make it as quiet as possible out of reverence to God and respect for the neighbors.

DID YOU KNOW King Solomon was also known by the name Jedidiah?

> She gave birth to a son, and they named him Solomon. The Lord loved him; and because the Lord loved him, he sent word through Nathan the prophet to name him Jedidiah.
>
> 2 Samuel 12:24–25

Why two names? Why not? The name means "God loves him" and was given to Solomon by God. Wouldn't you love it if God gave you a name like that?

DID YOU KNOW it took seven years to build God's temple, but it took 13 years to build Solomon's own palace?

> In the eleventh year in the month of Bul, the eighth month, the temple was finished in all its details according to its specifications. He had spent seven years building it.
>
> 1 Kings 6:38

> It took Solomon thirteen years, however, to complete the construction of his palace.
>
> 1 Kings 7:1

Hmmm . . . is there something wrong with this picture? While Solomon built the temple (God's house) first (that's good), he spent more time on his own house (that's bad)!

DID YOU KNOW King Solomon had 700 wives? That's a lot of anniversaries to remember!

> He had seven hundred wives of royal birth . . . and his wives led him astray.
>
> 1 Kings 11:3

God did not want Solomon to marry so many women, but Solomon thought it was a good idea to marry women of royal birth—the daughters of kings from other nations so that the other kings would not invade Israel. While these marriages may have been for a good reason, Solomon's wives brought their foreign gods to Jerusalem and caused King Solomon to eventually worship them.

DID YOU KNOW **King David received a prophecy about Jesus 1,000 years before Christ was born?** A prophet named Nathan visited David and said this:

> Your house and your kingdom will endure forever before me; your throne will be established forever.
>
> 2 Samuel 7:16

What did that mean? It meant a king would come from the line of David who would rule forever. Both of Jesus' genealogies (Matthew and Luke) point out that David was Jesus' great-great-great-great-great-grandfather. Jesus is the one true king, and His kingdom will last for eternity.

DID YOU KNOW **Elijah invited 850 prophets to Mount Carmel for a showdown, but only 450 showed up?**

> Now summon the people from all over Israel to meet me on Mount Carmel. And bring the four hundred and fifty prophets of Baal and the four hundred prophets of Asherah, who eat at Jezebel's table.
>
> 1 Kings 18:19

When Elijah challenged his God to their god in a fire challenge, only 450 prophets of Baal showed up. Where did the 400 prophets of Asherah go? Probably "got lost" on the way there, or some other excuse, because they knew they didn't have a chance against the one true God!

DID YOU KNOW King David's son Absalom had really heavy hair? The Bible said it weighed 5 pounds, or 200 shekels (2 Samuel 14:26) when it was cut. Absalom had some strong neck muscles!

DID YOU KNOW that Nehemiah completed the wall around Jerusalem in 52 days? When Nehemiah led the exiles back into Jerusalem to rebuild the city, he managed to encourage the civilians to work quickly and efficiently despite opposition.

DID YOU KNOW that a holiday started by Queen Esther is still celebrated by Jews today? Purim commemorates the day when Esther helped save the Israelites in Persia from mass extinction. Traditionally the holiday occurs in March. People listen to readings in the synagogue, eat, give gifts, and help the poor.

DID YOU KNOW a cupbearer would taste the king's drink before the king sipped it? If the cupbearer didn't die, that meant the drink was not poisoned. This was history's first Secret Service job—a person willing to die for the sake of a king. Because of the cupbearer's sacrifice, the king respected the cupbearer greatly, which is probably why King Artaxerxes granted Nehemiah's wish to return to Jerusalem to help rebuild it. He trusted him.

DID YOU KNOW some think the Bible describes a dragon? God wanted Job to understand His power over all creation and described a beast called a Leviathan. The name means—get this—a sea monster, dragon, or large aquatic beast. When you read this passage in Job 41, you have to wonder . . .

> I will not fail to speak of Leviathan's limbs,
>   its strength and its graceful form.
> Who can strip off its outer coat?
>   Who can penetrate its double coat of armor?

Who dares open the doors of its mouth,
    ringed about with fearsome teeth?
Its back has rows of shields
    tightly sealed together;
each is so close to the next
    that no air can pass between.
They are joined fast to one another;
    they cling together and cannot be parted.
Its snorting throws out flashes of light;
    its eyes are like the rays of dawn.
Flames stream from its mouth;
    sparks of fire shoot out.
Smoke pours from its nostrils
    as from a boiling pot over burning reeds.
Its breath sets coals ablaze,
    and flames dart from its mouth.
Strength resides in its neck;
    dismay goes before it.
The folds of its flesh are tightly joined;
    they are firm and immovable.
Its chest is hard as rock,
    hard as a lower millstone.
When it rises up, the mighty are terrified;
    they retreat before its thrashing.
The sword that reaches it has no effect,
    nor does the spear or the dart or the javelin.
Iron it treats like straw
    and bronze like rotten wood.
Arrows do not make it flee;
    slingstones are like chaff to it.
A club seems to it but a piece of straw;
    it laughs at the rattling of the lance.

Job 41:12–29

Is it a dragon? Dragons are mythological creations. They do not exist. So what could this sea-dwelling (or possibly amphibious) creature be? Some think it might have been a whale, a crocodile, or a dinosaur.

Whatever it was, God wanted to make the point . . . whatever large, seemingly untamable creature walks on this earth, He can subdue it. And if it were a dragon, then God's the original dragon slayer!

DID YOU KNOW that some think the Bible also describes a dinosaur? Many believe the "Behemoth" God talks about in Job was a dinosaur. Read this passage in Job 40.

> Look at Behemoth,
>> which I made along with you
>> and which feeds on grass like an ox.
> What strength it has in its loins,
>> what power in the muscles of its belly!
> Its tail sways like a cedar;
>> the sinews of its thighs are close-knit.
> Its bones are tubes of bronze,
>> its limbs like rods of iron.
> It ranks first among the works of God,
>> yet its Maker can approach it with his sword.
> The hills bring it their produce,
>> and all the wild animals play nearby.
> Under the lotus plants it lies,
>> hidden among the reeds in the marsh.
> The lotuses conceal it in their shadow;
>> the poplars by the stream surround it.
> A raging river does not alarm it;
>> it is secure, though the Jordan should surge
>>> against its mouth.
> Can anyone capture it by the eyes,
>> or trap it and pierce its nose?
>
> Job 40:15–24

If it were a dinosaur, then it would be a plant eater, something along the lines of a brontosaurus.

Others feel it could be another animal like a hippo, an elephant, or a rhino. However, one description—"its tail sways like a cedar"—discounts these animals. Each of those above animals have tiny tails. The dinosaur, especially the brontosaurus, had huge, log-like tails.

DID YOU KNOW there are three constellations mentioned in the Bible? And all of them are mentioned in the book of Job . . .

> Can you bind the chains of the Pleiades?
>   Can you loosen Orion's belt?
> Can you bring forth the constellations in their seasons
>   or lead out the Bear with its cubs?
>
> Job 38:31–32

- ▶ Pleiades—also known as the constellation Taurus, consists of seven stars.
- ▶ Orion's belt—three stars close together line up in nearly a straight line to form part of the Orion constellation.
- ▶ The Bear—a seven-star constellation also known as the Bear, Ursa Major, or the Big Dipper.

DID YOU KNOW the name *Joshua* and *Jesus* are pretty much the same name? The Hebrew name of Joshua is *Jehoshua*, which means "the Lord is salvation." The Greek version of Joshua is Jesus and means the same thing. Jesus is our salvation, saving us from our sins. While Joshua saved the Israelites and helped them enter the Promised Land, Jesus helps us get into the real Promised Land: heaven.

DID YOU KNOW the longest name in the Bible is Maher-Shalal-Hash-Baz, the second son of Isaiah? His name means "to hurry and get the enemies' stuff after they've been conquered." Well, you can't be in a hurry saying a name like that!

DID YOU KNOW the word *meaningless* appears 35 times in the 12 chapters of Ecclesiastes? The word is also translated as "vanity" and means "just a breath, a vapor" that passes very quickly and then is gone. The writer, Solomon, wanted readers to know that the many pursuits in life were worth nothing compared to knowing God.

DID YOU KNOW that when some Israelites were burying a man, he came to life? The dead man's body touched Elisha's bones, which were in the cave, and the man sprung alive! (2 Kings 13:21) That's a "bone-ified" miracle!

DID YOU KNOW the Bible contains 66 books?

- 39 in the Old Testament
- 27 in the New Testament

How can you remember that? Thirty-nine (Old Testament) has the numbers 3 and 9; 3 x 9 = 27 (New Testament). You're welcome.

DID YOU KNOW that five nations invaded Israel and took them over during the time of the Bible?

- The Assyrians invade the Northern Kingdom of Israel in 722 BC.
- The Babylonians attacked in three waves (605, 597, and 586 BC) and ultimately Jerusalem fell.
- The Persians conquer Babylon in 539 BC with King Cyrus of Persia. The Jews were eventually allowed to return to Jerusalem.
- The Greeks conquered the Persians in 332 BC and took over Israel. This is not mentioned in the Bible because it happened between Malachi and the arrival of Jesus.
- The Romans conquered the Greeks in 63 BC and took over all the land the Greeks owned. When Jesus arrived on earth, the Romans were in charge of Israel.

DID YOU KNOW that the shortest book in the Old Testament is Obadiah? The shortest book of the New Testament is 3 John if you count words, or 2 John if you count verses. In terms of words, 3 John is the shortest book of the Bible.

DID YOU KNOW that the longest verse in the Bible is Esther 8:9? Seventy-one words!

DID YOU KNOW that the original king-sized bed was founded by an evil king named Og in the Bible?

Og king of Bashan was the last of the Rephaites. His bed was decorated with iron and was more than nine cubits long and four cubits wide. It is still in Rabbah of the Ammonites.

Deuteronomy 3:11

According to those measurements, it was about 13 to 14 feet long and 6 feet wide.

DID YOU KNOW there was a left-handed army in the Bible?

Among all these soldiers there were seven hundred select troops who were left-handed, each of whom could sling a stone at a hair and not miss.

Judges 20:16

Must have been hard for them to open a can of beans with no left-handed can openers around.

DID YOU KNOW David's nephew killed a man who had 12 fingers and 12 toes?

> In still another battle, which took place at Gath, there was a huge man with six fingers on each hand and six toes on each foot—twenty-four in all. He also was descended from Rapha. When he taunted Israel, Jonathan son of Shimeah, David's brother, killed him.
>
> 2 Samuel 21:20–21

While having 24 digits helps you to count higher, it obviously doesn't make you a better warrior.

DID YOU KNOW that the sun stood still for an entire day in the Bible? While Joshua fought the Amorites, the Bible said this:

> On the day the Lord gave the Amorites over to Israel, Joshua
>   said to the Lord in the presence of Israel:
> "Sun, stand still over Gibeon,
>   and you, moon, over the Valley of Aijalon."
> So the sun stood still,
>   and the moon stopped,
>   till the nation avenged itself on its enemies,
> as it is written in the Book of Jashar.
> The sun stopped in the middle of the sky and delayed going
>   down about a full day. There has never been a day like it
>   before or since, a day when the Lord listened to a human
>   being. Surely the Lord was fighting for Israel!
>
> Joshua 10:12–14

That's a long day! Like two days in one.

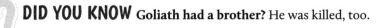

DID YOU KNOW **Goliath had a brother?** He was killed, too.

In another battle with the Philistines at Gob, Elhanan son of Jair the Bethlehemite killed the brother of Goliath the Gittite, who had a spear with a shaft like a weaver's rod.

2 Samuel 21:19

Those Goliaths did not have a very pleasant family reunion.

DID YOU KNOW **that the prophet Hosea married a woman named Gomer?** The name in Hebrew means "complete." Not a completely popular name among women today.

DID YOU KNOW **that God asked the prophet Hosea to name his kids Jezreel (I-Will-Punish), Lo-ruhamah (Not-Loved), and Lo-ammi (Not-My-People)?** These are pretty sad names for kids, but God wanted to remind them all the time about Israel's separation from God. Aren't you glad your parents gave you the name you have instead of names like Hosea's kids?

DID YOU KNOW **the Bible knew where Jesus would be born 700 years before His birth?**

But you, Bethlehem Ephrathah,
    though you are small among the clans of Judah,
out of you will come for me
    one who will be ruler over Israel,
whose origins are from of old,
    from ancient times.

Micah 5:2

Matthew remembered this verse and mentioned it in chapter 2:6 when talking about the birth of Jesus.

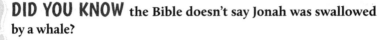

DID YOU KNOW the Bible doesn't say Jonah was swallowed by a whale?

> Now the Lord provided a huge fish to swallow Jonah, and Jonah was in the belly of the fish three days and three nights.
>
> Jonah 1:17

What kind of big fish was it? There are whales in the Mediterranean Sea—the fin whale and the sperm whale. There are also many sharks, including the great white, that swim in this sea. Jonah could have met the original Jaws.

DID YOU KNOW that angels have six wings? When Isaiah saw the angels in chapter 6, verse 2, he said two wings covered their faces, two covered their feet, and two were flying. Why did the angels cover their faces and feet? These are ways to show humility to someone greater, communicating that the angels felt they could not look at God or show Him their feet.

DID YOU KNOW that only two angels in the Bible have names? Gabriel and Michael. Both of them appear in both the Old and New Testament.

Gabriel is found in Daniel 8 and 9 when he speaks to Daniel regarding images and prophecy. Gabriel then announces to Mary that she would give birth to the Messiah.

Michael appears in Daniel 10 and 12, and he's also speaking about prophecies and the end times. He is mentioned in two New Testament books, Titus and Revelation.

While there are millions of angels, only these two get recognized by name. They rank high in the angelic army, meaning they have leadership positions in the ranks.

DID YOU KNOW that when Shadrach, Meshach, and Abednego were put into the fiery furnace, the king saw a fourth person? King Nebuchadnezzar said he saw four men walking around, and the fourth looked like a "son of the gods." Who was this fourth man? Some believe an angel. Some think Jesus himself, the Son of God. The fire did not burn one hair on their head or one stitch of their clothing. They didn't even smell like fire! Whoever was in there with them kept them safe.

DID YOU KNOW that the Magi's gifts to Jesus were all mentioned in the same chapter of Exodus? In Exodus 30, *gold* was part of the altar of incense, *myrrh* was an ingredient in the anointing oil for the priests, and *frankincense* was used for the incense burned at the temple. The gifts signify Jesus' importance as a sacrifice to fulfill what the temple/tabernacle tried to do.

DID YOU KNOW the tabernacle was a portable temple? Moses used the tabernacle in the wilderness to perform sacrifices. It had to be dismantled and reassembled when God moved them from place to place for 40 years. Kind of like many churches who set up in schools and auditoriums every Sunday. Church in a box!

DID YOU KNOW that Solomon built a throne room called the Hall of Justice? It's the same name the Super Friends—Batman, Superman, Wonder Woman, and Aquaman—call their headquarters.

DID YOU KNOW King Uzziah made devices that he mounted on his towers that shot arrows and hurled large stones? These catapults and arrow launchers were powerful war weapons that made him well-known and very powerful to his enemies.

DID YOU KNOW **India is mentioned in the Bible?** King Xerxes, from the book of Esther, ruled from India to Cush (also known as Egypt). Spain is mentioned in the New Testament, where Paul wanted to visit during his journeys. No mention of Canada.

DID YOU KNOW **God is never mentioned in the book of Esther?** Because of that, many early church scholars wanted the book removed. However, it is clearly seen that God was working behind the scenes to save the lives of the Jews while they lived in Persia.

DID YOU KNOW **there's a city in *Star Wars* that uses a name from the Bible?** In 1 Samuel 28, King Saul paid a medium (someone who contacts the dead) to help him. That woman lived in Endor. In *Star Wars: Return of the Jedi*, Endor is a Forest Moon and home of the Ewoks. May the Holy Spirit be with you!

THE SHEPHERD IS
at a LOSS for WORDS

Psalm 23, the most famous Psalm of them all, is incomplete without the right words. Put the words in the correct places to complete the Psalm.

Staff	Soul	Waters
Love	Shepherd	Cup
Pastures	Valley	Paths
House	Table	Oil

The Lord is my _____, I lack nothing.

He makes me lie down in green _____,

he leads me beside quiet _____,

he refreshes my _____.

He guides me along the right _____
for his name's sake.

Even though I walk

through the darkest _____,

I will fear no evil,
for you are with me;

your rod and your _____,

    they comfort me.

You prepare a _____ before me

    in the presence of my enemies.

You anoint my head with _____;

    my _____ overflows.

Surely your goodness and _____ will follow me
    all the days of my life,

and I will dwell in the _____ of the Lord
    forever.

Answers:

The Lord is my **shepherd**, I lack nothing.
He makes me lie down in green **pastures**,
he leads me beside quiet **waters**,
    he refreshes my **soul**.
He guides me along the right **paths**
    for his name's sake.
Even though I walk
through the darkest **valley**,
    I will **fear** no evil,
for you are with me;
your rod and your **staff**,
    they comfort me.
You prepare a **table** before me
in the presence of my enemies.
You anoint my head with **oil**;
    my **cup** overflows.
Surely your goodness and **love** will follow me
all the days of my life,
and I will dwell in the **house** of the Lord
    forever.

SEEK and YOU WiLL FiND

The Ites Have It

The suffix "ites" was added to a country's name to reference the people from that area. For example, those from Israel were called Israelites. Circle the "ites" that are found in the Bible and ignore the ones that are just trying to fool you.

Perizzites	Jebusites	Horites
Amalekites	Maakathites	Woolites
Appetites	Frostbites	Sinites
Arkites	Girzites	Satellites
Canaanites	Kadmonites	Stalactites
Cellulites	Kenites	Zuzites
Finites	Gittites	Zebusites
Kenizzites	Parasites	Emites
Socialites	Amorites	Websites
Geshurites	Rephaites	Zamzummites
Hittites	Samsonites	
Hivites	Gibeonites	

Answers: Perizzites, Amalekites, Arkites, Canaanites, Kenizzites, Geshurites, Hittites, Hivites, Jebusites, Maakathites, Girzites, Kadmonites, Kenites, Gittites, Amorites, Rephaites, Gibeonites, Horites, Sinites, Zuzites, Zebusites, Emites, Zamzummites

Where in the World?

Circle six cities from the list below that are found in the United States and are also mentioned as places in the Bible.

Salem	Seattle
Houston	Omaha
Portland	Phoenix
Philadelphia	Boise
Orlando	Bethlehem
Birmingham	Sacramento
Memphis	Reno
Syracuse	Tulsa

Answers:

Salem—Mentioned in Genesis 14:18 as a town Abraham visited. Later, that town became Jeru-salem, which means "peace." Today found in Massachusetts.

Philadelphia—One of the cities of Revelation, which John addressed in Revelation 3. The name means "brotherly love." Today found in Pennsylvania.

Memphis—Mentioned in Isaiah, Jeremiah, Ezekiel, and Hosea. Today found in Tennessee.

Syracuse—Mentioned in Acts 28:12 as a place Paul visited on his journeys. Today found in New York.

Phoenix—Mentioned in Acts 27:12 as a place Paul hoped to reach on one of his journeys. Today found in Arizona.

Bethlehem—The town where David and Jesus were born. Today found in Pennsylvania.

Jacob's Very Busy Father's Day

Circle the twelve sons of Jacob.

Zebulun	Naphtali
Jehoshaphat	Josiah
Reuben	James
Ephraim	Judah
Malachi	Zerubbabel
Levi	Dan
Saul	Nicodemus
John	Joseph
Simeon	Jeremiah
Cyrus	Asa
Asher	Isaiah
Ezra	Benjamin
Zophar	Uzziah
Issachar	Gad

Answers: In birth order: Reuben, Simeon, Levi, Judah, Dan, Naphtali, Gad, Asher, Issachar, Zebulun, Joseph, Benjamin

Follow the Rules

Which of these are real laws mentioned in the book of Leviticus? (And the others are things your mom probably tells you.)

A. Don't jump on the bed.

B. Don't curse the deaf.

C. Don't trip the blind.

D. Don't sweep dirt under the rug.

E. Remove mold from your house.

F. Don't jump on your brother.

G. Don't plant your field with two kinds of seeds.

H. Don't jump off a cliff even if everyone else is doing it.

I. Don't wear clothing made of two materials.

J. Don't talk with your mouth full.

K. Don't practice witchcraft.

L. Eat your vegetables.

M. Don't clip the edges of your beard.

N. Always make your bed.

O. Don't cry over spilled milk.

P. Stand up when older people come into your presence.

Q. Close the door unless you live in a barn.

R. Don't eat bloody meat.

S. Always put a napkin on your lap when it's time to eat.

Answers: B, C, E, G, I, K, M, P, R

To Sacrifice or Not to Sacrifice

Which of these animals were sacrificed according to the Old Testament law so people could be forgiven of their sins? Circle the animals that the book of Leviticus specifically said could be offered.

Buffalo	Dove
Bull	Pigeon
Pig	Sparrow
Peacock	Ram
Sheep	Lamb
Goat	Ostrich
Rooster	

Answers: bull, sheep, goat, dove, pigeon, ram, lamb

Bible Holy Days

Which of these are real festivals that the Israelites were told to celebrate in the Old Testament?

Festival of Tabernacles	Christmas
Festival of Trees	Carnaval
Festival of Trumpets	Boxing Day
Arbor Day	Day of Silence
Black Friday	Day of Atonement
Festival of Weeks	St. Patrick's Day
Passover	Cinco de Mayo

Answers:
Festival of Tabernacles (Feast of Tabernacles or Feast of Booths or Sukkot)
Festival of Trumpets (Feast of Trumpets or Rosh Hashanah)
Festival of Weeks (Feast of Weeks, Shavuot, or Pentecost)
Passover
Day of Atonement (Yom Kippur)

Here Come the Judges

Which of these were judges who God used to protect His people in the book of Judges?

Stallone	Schwarzenegger
Othniel	Shamgar
Ibzan	Ehud
Jephthah	Jair
Hezekiah	The Hulk
Han Solo	Deborah
Elon	Gideon
Abdon	Tola
Samson	Gandolf

Answers: Othniel, Ibzan, Jephthah, Elon, Abdon, Samson, Shamgar, Ehud, Jair, Deborah, Gideon, Tola

The Fashion Priests

In the Old Testament, the priests of the temple wore a very specific fashion, designed by God. Circle the items that were part of their attire.

Tunic	Pants
Cuff links	Waistband
Sash	Breastpiece
Earrings	Turban
Robe	Socks
Nose guard	Suspenders
Ephod	Undergarments

Answers: tunic, ephod, waistband, sash, breastpiece, robe, turban, undergarments

Join the Band

The Bible mentions a lot of instruments. Circle the musical instruments that you can read about in the Bible.

Harp	Trumpet
Drum	Bassoon
Lyre	Flute
Pipe	Bells
Tuba	Xylophone
Saxophone	Castanet
Timbrel	Cymbals
Ram's Horn	Kazoo
Air Guitar	

Fruit Hunters

Which of these fruits are mentioned in the Bible? (Hint: there are only six)

Apple	Pomegranate
Cherry	Date
Banana	Apricot
Fig	Strawberry
Mango	Strawberry
Grape	Lemon
Pineapple	Olive
	Orange

Answers: apple, fig, grape, pomegranate, date, olive

THOSE ANiMALS ARE SO SMART

Proverbs contains a number of wise sayings. Put the right animal into the right saying to understand the wisdom of Proverbs.

Oxen	Horse	Pig	Gazelle
Lizard	Leech	Donkey	Lion
Ant	Ravens	Locusts	
Bear	Dog	Eagle	

A. Free yourself, like a _____ from the hand of the hunter. . . . (Proverbs 6:5)

B. Go to the _____, you sluggard; consider its ways and be wise! (Proverbs 6:6)

C. Like a gold ring in a _____'s snout is a beautiful woman who shows no discretion. (Proverbs 11:22)

D. Where there are no _____, the manger is empty. (Proverbs 14:4)

E. Better to meet a _____ robbed of her cubs than a fool bent on folly. (Proverbs 17:12)

F. A king's rage is like the roar of a _____, but his favor is like dew on the grass. (Proverbs 19:12)

G. The _____ is made ready for the day of battle, but victory rests with the Lord. (Proverbs 21:31)

H. Riches . . . will surely sprout wings and fly off to the sky like an _____. (Proverbs 23:5)

I. A whip for the horse, a bridle for the _____, and a rod for the backs of fools! (Proverbs 26:3)

J. As a _____ returns to its vomit, so fools repeat their folly. (Proverbs 26:11)

K. The _____ has two daughters, "Give, Give" they cry. (Proverbs 30:15)

L. The eye that mocks a father, that scorns an aged mother, will be pecked out by the _____. (Proverbs 30:17)

M. _____ have no king, yet they advance together in ranks. (Proverbs 30:27)

N. A _____ can be caught with the hand, yet it is found in kings' palaces. (Proverbs 30:28)

Answers:

A. gazelle	E. bear	I. donkey	M. locusts
B. ant	F. lion	J. dog	N. lizard
C. pig	G. horse	K. leech	
D. oxen	H. eagle	L. ravens	

THAT'S FROM the BiBLE?

So many popular phrases that we use today originated from the Bible. Have you ever heard of these?

A drop in a bucket. "Surely the nations are like a drop in a bucket; they are regarded as dust on the scales; he weighs the islands as though they were fine dust" (Isaiah 40:15).

A house divided against itself cannot stand. "If a house is divided against itself, that house cannot stand" (Mark 3:25).

A leopard cannot change his spots. "Can an Ethiopian change his skin or a leopard its spots? Neither can you do good who are accustomed to doing evil" (Jeremiah 13:23).

Apple of his eye. "Keep me as the apple of your eye; hide me in the shadow of your wings" (Psalm 17:8).

As white as snow. "Cleanse me with hyssop, and I will be clean; wash me, and I will be whiter than snow" (Psalm 51:7).

A wolf in sheep's clothing. "Watch out for false prophets. They come to you in sheep's clothing, but inwardly they are ferocious wolves" (Matthew 7:15).

My brother's keeper. "Then the Lord said to Cain, 'Where is your brother Abel?' 'I don't know,' he replied. 'Am I my brother's keeper?'" (Genesis 4:9).

Blind leading the blind. "Leave them; they are blind guides. If the blind lead the blind, both will fall into a pit" (Matthew 15:14).

By the skin of your teeth. "I am nothing but skin and bones; I have escaped only by the skin of my teeth" (Job 19:20).

By the sweat of your brow. "By the sweat of your brow you will eat your food until you return to the ground, since from it you were taken; for dust you are and to dust you will return" (Genesis 3:19).

Eat, drink, and be merry. "And I'll say to myself, 'You have plenty of grain laid up for many years. Take life easy; eat, drink and be merry'" (Luke 12:19).

Eye for an eye. "If there is serious injury, you are to take life for life, eye for eye, tooth for tooth, hand for hand, foot for foot. . . ." (Exodus 21:23–24).

Fight the good fight. "Fight the good fight of the faith. Take hold of the eternal life to which you were called when you made your good confession in the presence of many witnesses" (1 Timothy 6:12).

The first will be last and the last will be first. "Don't I have the right to do what I want with my own money? Or are you envious because I am generous? 'So the last will be first, and the first will be last'" (Matthew 20:15–16).

Go the extra mile. "If anyone forces you to go one mile, go with them two miles" (Matthew 5:41).

He who is without sin, cast the first stone. "When they kept on questioning him, he straightened up and said to them, 'Let any one of you who is without sin be the first to throw a stone at her'" (John 8:7).

He who lives by the sword will die by the sword. "Then Jesus told him, 'Put your sword back in its place because all who take up a sword will perish by a sword'" (Matthew 26:52 HCSB).

In the twinkling of an eye. "In a flash, in the twinkling of an eye, at the last trumpet. For the trumpet will sound, the dead will be raised imperishable, and we will be changed" (1 Corinthians 15:52).

It's better to give than to receive. "In everything I did, I showed you that by this kind of hard work we must help the weak, remembering the words the Lord Jesus himself said: 'It is more blessed to give than to receive'" (Acts 20:35).

Money is the root of all evil. "For the love of money is a root of all kinds of evil. Some people, eager for money, have wandered from the faith and pierced themselves with many griefs" (1 Timothy 6:10).

Love your neighbor as yourself. "The second is this: 'Love your neighbor as yourself.' There is no commandment greater than these" (Mark 12:31).

Many are called but few are chosen. "For many are called, but few are chosen" (Matthew 22:14 KJV).

My cup runneth over. "Thou preparest a table before me in the presence of mine enemies: thou anointest my head with oil; my cup runneth over" (Psalm 23:5 KJV).

No rest for the wicked. "But the wicked are like the tossing sea, which cannot rest, whose waves cast up mire and mud" (Isaiah 57:20).

Out of the mouths of babes. "Out of the mouth of babes and nursing infants You have ordained strength, Because of Your enemies, That You may silence the enemy and the avenger" (Psalm 8:2 NKJV).

Pride goes before the fall. "Pride goes before destruction, a haughty spirit before a fall" (Proverbs 16:18).

Sign of the times. "'Today it will be stormy, for the sky is red and overcast.' You know how to interpret the appearance of the sky, but you cannot interpret the signs of the times" (Matthew 16:3).

The spirit is willing but the flesh is weak. "Watch and pray so that you will not fall into temptation. The spirit is willing, but the flesh is weak" (Mark 14:38).

The writing is on the wall. "Suddenly the fingers of a human hand appeared and wrote on the plaster of the wall, near the lampstand in the royal palace. The king watched the hand as it wrote" (Daniel 5:5).

Thorn in my side. "Therefore, in order to keep me from becoming conceited, I was given a thorn in my flesh, a messenger of Satan, to torment me" (2 Corinthians 12:7).

You'll reap what you sow. "Do not be deceived: God cannot be mocked. A man reaps what he sows" (Galatians 6:7).

You of little faith. "He replied, 'You of little faith, why are you so afraid?' Then he got up and rebuked the winds and the waves, and it was completely calm" (Matthew 8:26).

GOD DiD THAT

When Job and his friends talked about the reason for Job's problems, God stepped in and questioned how they could understand His ways. In Job 38–41, He listed all the things that He has done, an impressive résumé of creation.

GOD . . .

- ▸ Laid the earth's foundation
- ▸ Laid out the seas
- ▸ Designed the clouds
- ▸ Orders the morning and dawn
- ▸ Gave the earth its shape
- ▸ Punishes the wicked
- ▸ Journeyed into the deep sea
- ▸ Has seen the gates of death
- ▸ Has seen the whole earth
- ▸ Knows where light and darkness reside
- ▸ Knows where snow, hailstorms, lightning, wind, rain, and ice begin
- ▸ Designed the constellations
- ▸ Knows the laws of heaven and earth
- ▸ Sends lightning bolts
- ▸ Gives the ibis (a bird) and rooster wisdom
- ▸ Counts the clouds
- ▸ Takes care of lions and knows what they are doing

- ▸ Feeds ravens
- ▸ Knows when mountain goats and deer give birth
- ▸ Lets donkeys run free
- ▸ Tames the oxen
- ▸ Knows what ostriches are up to
- ▸ Gives horses their strength
- ▸ Made eagles and hawks to fly, nest, and hunt
- ▸ Made the Behemoth and can tame it
- ▸ Made the Leviathan and can tame it

Are you impressed?

WHAT TiME IS IT?

The writer of Ecclesiastes talks about time, especially in chapter 3. Match the right time in the right place. (HINT: The missing word in the sentence is [usually] the opposite of the other word in the sentence.)

Throw away	Silent	Dance
Peace	Build	Born
Scatter	Heal	Search
Uproot	Love	Laugh

There is a time for everything,
  and a season for every activity under the heavens:

  a time to be _____ and a time to die,

  a time to plant and a time to _____,

  a time to kill and a time to _____,

  a time to tear down and a time to _____,

  a time to weep and a time to _____,

  a time to mourn and a time to _____,

  a time to _____ stones and a time to
    gather them,

a time to embrace and a time to refrain from embracing,

a time to _____ and a time to give up,

a time to keep and a time to _____,

a time to tear and a time to mend,

a time to be _____ and a time to speak,

a time to _____ and a time to hate,

a time for war and a time for _____.

WISE or FOOL, YOU DECIDE

Circle the word "Wise" if Proverbs calls this kind of action wise, or "Fool" if Proverbs calls this kind of action a fool.

A. Brings joy to his father — WISE / FOOL

B. Brings grief to his mother — WISE / FOOL

C. Listens to advice — WISE / FOOL

D. Talks all the time — WISE / FOOL

E. Winks maliciously — WISE / FOOL

F. Takes crooked paths — WISE / FOOL

G. Stores up knowledge — WISE / FOOL

H. Invites ruin and poverty into their life — WISE / FOOL

I. Ignores correction — WISE / FOOL

J. Holds their tongue — WISE / FOOL

K. Spreads gossip — WISE / FOOL

L. Will only inherit wind — WISE / FOOL

M. Their way seems right to them — WISE / FOOL

N. Their lips protect them — WISE / FOOL

O. Quick tempered   WISE / FOOL

P. Plans fail   WISE / FOOL

Q. Has many advisors   WISE / FOOL

R. Their words like choice morsels   WISE / FOOL

S. Loves life   WISE / FOOL

T. Loves to sleep   WISE / FOOL

U. Stores up their food   WISE / FOOL

V. Gulps down their food   WISE / FOOL

W. Drinks too much   WISE / FOOL

X. Confesses sin   WISE / FOOL

Y. Conceals their sin   WISE / FOOL

Z. Trusts in themselves   WISE / FOOL

Answers:

A. Wise	H. Fool	N. Wise	U. Wise
B. Fool	I. Fool	M. Fool	T. Fool
C. Wise	J. Wise	L. Fool	S. Wise	Z. Fool
D. Fool	K. Fool	R. Wise	Y. Fool
E. Fool	L. Fool	Q. Wise	X. Wise
F. Fool	M. Fool	P. Fool	W. Fool
G. Wise	N. Wise	O. Fool	V. Fool

SO YOU WANT to BE a PROPHET?

Being a prophet was tough; God asked His prophets to do some difficult stuff. Read these things God asked them to do and ask yourself... *Would I want to be a prophet?*

1. Isaiah walked around **naked** for three years to show everyone a sign for what God would do to other nations. (Isaiah 20:3)

2. Hosea was asked to **marry** a woman who would be unfaithful to him. (Hosea 1:2–3)

3. Jonah was told to go into **enemy territory** and tell everyone God was mad at them. No wonder he ran away! (Jonah 1:1–3)

4. Jeremiah was told to go buy a linen **belt** and bury it in the rocks. Then days later he was to dig it up, and he found it ruined. That was a brand-new belt! (Jeremiah 13:1–7)

5. Jeremiah was told **not to marry** or have kids since life in Judah was going to get so bad. (Jeremiah 16:1)

6. Jeremiah had to walk around town with a **yoke** around his neck. The yokes on you! (Jeremiah 27:2)

7. Jeremiah was thrown into a **cistern**, an underground water tank. (Jeremiah 38:6)

8. Daniel was thrown into a den with **lions**. (Daniel 6:16)

9. Ezekiel had to lay on his side and look at a model of **Jerusalem** for 430 days. (Ezekiel 4:5–6) That sounds pretty boring.

10. Ezekiel had to eat a loaf of **bread** baked over cow doo-doo. (Ezekiel 4:15)

11. God told Ezekiel to give himself a haircut with a **sword**. (Ezekiel 5:1)

12. God told Ezekiel that his **wife** would die, but not to mourn for her. (Ezekiel 24:16–18)

NEW TESTAMENT SCRAMBLE

Unscramble these letters to find books in the New Testament. (Note: For those that are first or second books, we removed the number and focused only on the book name.)

1. Wet Math

2. Cats

3. No Arms

4. Act in rhinos

5. Tag a snail

6. Shine peas

7. Hip slip pain

8. Coins lasso

9. Tan as holiness

10. Hi my tot

11. Hip melon

12. Her webs

13. In elevator

THE GOSPEL of ZOOLOGY

Jesus talked about animals all the time. Fill in the blanks with the right animal Jesus talked about.

Camel	Donkey	Goats
Lambs	Pigs	Dogs
Snake	Oxen	Fish
Rooster	Birds	Foxes

1. Do not give dogs what is sacred; do not throw your pearls to _____. If you do, they may trample them under their feet, and turn and tear you to pieces. (Matthew 7:6)

2. Or if he asks for a fish, will give him a _____? (Matthew 7:10)

3. Jesus replied, "_____ have dens and birds have nests, but the Son of Man has no place to lay his head" (Matthew 8:20).

4. Go to the village ahead of you, and at once you will find a _____ tied there, with her colt by her. Untie them and bring them to me. (Matthew 21:2)

5. He will put the sheep on his right and the _____ on his left. (Matthew 25:33)

6. "Come, follow me," Jesus said, "and I will send you out to _____ for people" (Mark 1:17).

7. As he was scattering the seed, some fell along the path, and the _____ came and ate it up. (Mark 4:4)

8. "First let the children eat all they want," he told her, "for it is not right to take the children's bread and toss it to the _____" (Mark 7:27).

9. Go! I am sending you out like _____ among wolves. (Luke 10:3)

10. Another said, "I have just bought five yoke of _____, and I'm on my way to try them out. Please excuse me" (Luke 14:19).

11. Indeed, it is easier for a _____ to go through the eye of a needle than for someone who is rich to enter the kingdom of God. (Luke 18:25)

12. Then Jesus answered, "Will you really lay down your life for me? Very truly I tell you, before the _____ crows, you will disown me three times!" (John 13:38).

Answers:

1. Pigs	4. Donkey	7. Birds	10. Oxen
2. Snake	5. Goats	8. Dogs	11. Camel
3. Foxes	6. Fish	9. Lambs	12. Rooster

DiD YOU KNOW? Part 2

DID YOU KNOW Jesus was probably two years old when the wise men visited Him? Herod calculated the time the wise men saw the star, and ordered all children two years and younger to be killed. When the wise men arrived in Bethlehem, they found Jesus, Mary, and Joseph in a house, not a manger.

DID YOU KNOW the gifts of gold, frankincense, and myrrh that the wise men brought Jesus and His family probably helped them financially as they escaped to Egypt? Without work and on the run from Herod, Joseph and his family needed money for food and shelter for almost five years in an unfamiliar land. They could sell the gold, frankincense, and myrrh to buy food.

DID YOU KNOW Joseph had four dreams that directed him to safely protect his family and Jesus? They were . . .

1. The angel in his dream told him to keep Mary as his wife and to name the baby Jesus. (Matthew 1:20)
2. The angel in his dream told him to go to Egypt to escape Herod. (Matthew 2:13)
3. The angel in his dream told him to return to Israel since Herod was dead. (Matthew 2:19)
4. The angel in his dream told him to go live in Nazareth. (Matthew 2:22–23)

DID YOU KNOW there are four books of the Bible that Paul wrote in prison? Many believe Paul penned Ephesians, Colossians, Philippians, and Philemon while he was in prison because in each of the books he used the phrase "in chains" to describe his current situation.

DID YOU KNOW why Peter's proclamation "You are the Messiah, the Son of the living God!" made Jesus so happy? Peter clearly believed three aspects of Jesus' identity that were all correct, and in order to properly know Jesus you must accept all three.

1. Messiah—Jesus was the prophesied savior clearly identified in the Old Testament, who came to save the people from their sins.
2. Son—Jesus is the Son of God.
3. Living God—Jesus is God and He's alive and well!

If you want to make Jesus happy, believe those three things about Him!

DID YOU KNOW why there were 12 apostles? Because there were 12 tribes of Israel. The 12 apostles were Jewish, and they were sent to take Jesus' message to the people of Israel. The number 12 brings the Old Testament and the New Testament together.
The apostles' names had to be confusing!

- Two named Simon (Mark 3:16, 18)
- Two named James (Mark 3:17, 18)
- Two named Judas (Luke 6:16)

No wonder Jesus changed one Simon's name to Peter!

DID YOU KNOW that Jesus spit on people?

▶ In Mark 7, Jesus spit on a man's tongue so he could speak.
▶ In Mark 8, Jesus spit in a man's eye to help him see.

While it sounds gross to have someone spit on you, Jesus' spit had miraculous powers!

DID YOU KNOW that the first convert to Christ in the continent of Asia was a man named Epenetus, according to Paul in Romans 16? Since then, many, many more have come to know Christ, but Epenetus started it all.

DID YOU KNOW that at least one of the apostles was married? We know for sure Peter was because in 1 Corinthians, Paul mentioned that Peter had a mother-in-law who Jesus healed.

DID YOU KNOW Paul told people in church to greet one another with a holy kiss? What's a holy kiss? Probably a respectful peck on the cheek exhibited in many Middle Eastern countries today. It's a "holy" kiss, meaning it's not done with romantic purposes but to show love and kindness to the one being kissed.

DID YOU KNOW that heaven will have streets of gold and pearly gates? "The twelve gates were twelve pearls, each gate made of a single pearl. The great street of the city was of gold, as pure as transparent glass" (Revelation 21:21).

The most precious items we have on earth will be nothing more than fences and pavement in heaven. The most valuable thing in heaven is God. Gold and pearls do not match up.

DID YOU KNOW that the gates of the great city in heaven are named after the tribes of Israel, and the foundations of the walls are named after the twelve apostles?

> It had a great, high wall with twelve gates, and with twelve angels at the gates. On the gates were written the names of the twelve tribes of Israel. There were three gates on the east, three on the north, three on the south and three on the west. The wall of the city had twelve foundations, and on them were the names of the twelve apostles of the Lamb.
>
> Revelation 21:12–14

Why is that? It's because heaven brings together the Old and New Testament. What the 12 tribes started in the Old Testament led to the message of the 12 apostles in the New Testament. All of their effort brought people into a relationship with God for eternity.

DID YOU KNOW Zacchaeus is the only person in the Bible who is called short?

Ehud (from the book of Judges) is the only person in the Bible who is described as left-handed, though there are soldiers mentioned who are left-handed.

Many are called tall. Two are called fat (King Eglon and Eli the priest). No one is called ugly.

DID YOU KNOW that the sign over Jesus' head on the cross was written in three languages: Aramaic, Latin, and Greek—the three most popular languages of the day? It was like God wanted everyone from every language to know what was written on it: "JESUS OF NAZARETH, THE KING OF THE JEWS."

DID YOU KNOW people started calling believers "Christians" in Antioch around the time of Acts 11? Originally the movement of Christianity was called "The Way" after Jesus' statement that He was the "the way, the truth and the life." The term *Christian* stuck.

DID YOU KNOW that the apostles picked a new apostle after Judas died? They chose between two candidates, Barsabbas and Matthias. Matthias won and made the number of apostles a perfect 12 once again. (Acts 1:23–26)

DID YOU KNOW there are many colorful horses in the Bible?
In Zechariah, the prophets saw red, white, brown, black, and dappled (spotted) horses.
In Revelation, John saw red, white, black, and pale horses.
Each of these colorful horses represented something different, but all of them meant something bad. So if you see a red, black, white, or pale horse riding toward you . . . run!

DID YOU KNOW that the last word of the Bible is *Amen*? (Revelation 22:21) The word translates to mean "so be it," "let it be so," or "truth." The perfect way to end the Word of God. Let it be so!

CAN'T SiNG IF YOU DON'T KNOW the WORDS Part 3

Fill in the missing word from these Psalms to complete the phrase. The right word makes all the difference.

> Lamp   Still   House
> Breath   Book   East

A. Be _____ before the Lord
   and wait patiently for him. (Psalm 37:7)

B. For as high as the heavens are above the earth,
   so great is his love for those who fear him;
   as far as the _____ is from the west,
   so far has he removed our transgressions from us.
   (Psalm 103:11–12)

C. Your word is a _____ for my feet,
   a light on my path. (Psalm 119:105)

D. Unless the Lord builds the _____,
   the builders labor in vain.
   Unless the Lord watches over the city,
   the guards stand watch in vain. (Psalm 127:1)

E. Your eyes saw my unformed body;
   all the days ordained for me were written in your

   _____

   before one of them came to be. (Psalm 139:16)

F. Let everything that has _____ praise the Lord.
   (Psalm 150:6)

BiBLE LiSTS

7 Amazing Facts About the Book of Psalms

1. It has the most chapters of any other book of the Bible: 150
2. It has the most verses of any other book of the Bible: 2,461
3. It has the longest chapter of any other book of the Bible: Psalm 119 (150 verses)
4. It has the shortest chapter of any other book of the Bible: Psalm 117
5. Psalm 118:8 is the middle of the Bible.
6. It has the most authors credited to its writing: 7
7. It is the most-quoted Old Testament book in the New Testament (over 60 times).

10 Shortest Books in the Bible by Chapters, Words, and Verses

1. 3 John—1 chapter, 14 verses, 299 words
2. 2 John—1 chapter, 13 verses, 303 words
3. Philemon—1 chapter, 25 verses, 445 words
4. Jude—1 chapter, 25 verses, 613 words
5. Obadiah—1 chapter, 21 verses, 670 words
6. Titus—3 chapters, 46 verses, 921 words

7. 2 Thessalonians—3 chapters, 47 verses, 1,042 words
8. Haggai—2 chapters, 38 verses, 1,131 words
9. Nahum—3 chapters, 47 verses, 1,285 words
10. Jonah—4 chapters, 48 verses, 1,321 words

10 Longest Books in the Bible by Chapters, Words, and Verses

1. Psalms—150 chapters, 2,461 verses, 43,743 words
2. Jeremiah—52 chapters, 1,364 verses, 42,659 words
3. Ezekiel—48 chapters, 1,273 verses, 39,407 words
4. Genesis—50 chapters, 1,533 verses, 38,267 words
5. Isaiah—66 chapters, 1,292 verses, 37,044 words
6. Numbers—36 chapters, 1,288 verses, 32,902 words
7. Exodus—40 chapters, 1,213 verses, 32,602 words
8. Deuteronomy—34 chapters, 959 verses, 28,461 words
9. 2 Chronicles—36 chapters, 822 verses, 26,074 words
10. Luke—24 chapters, 1,151 verses, 25,944 words

7 Authors Who Wrote the Book of Psalms

(100 psalms are credited; the other 50 are uncredited.)

1. King David is attributed with the most psalms: 73 in total
2. King Solomon, David's son, wrote two psalms: 72, 127
3. Asaph wrote 12 psalms: 50, 73–83
4. The Sons of Korah wrote 11 psalms: 42, 44–49, 84–85, 87, 88
5. Heman the Ezrahite shares credit on Psalm 88.
6. Ethan the Ezrahite is credited with Psalm 89.
7. Moses is credited with Psalm 90.

3 Writers of the Book of Proverbs

1. Proverbs was written primarily by King Solomon (or transcribed by his staff, who wrote down all the wise things he said).
2. Agur, son of Jakeh, wrote chapter 30.
3. King Lemuel wrote chapter 31.

Top 7 Prophecies in Isaiah About Jesus Christ

They were written 700 years before Jesus was born!

1. Isaiah 4:2–4 calls the Messiah a Branch who will cleanse the nation of their sins.
2. Isaiah 7:14 states the Messiah would be born of a virgin.
3. Isaiah 9:6 calls the child who would be born a Wonderful Counselor, Mighty God, Prince of Peace, Everlasting Father.
4. Isaiah 11:1–3 says this Branch will come from the family tree of Jesse (David), and the Spirit of God will rest on Him.
5. Isaiah 40:3 prophesizes the coming of John the Baptist, who would proclaim the coming of Jesus while living in the desert.
6. Isaiah 52:13–15 speaks of the Servant who will be disfigured beyond belief (Jesus on the cross).
7. Isaiah 53 gives amazing details into the crucifixion of Jesus. Read it yourself!

7 Parables Mentioned in 3 Gospels (none are mentioned in all 4)

1. Parable of the Light and Bowl
2. Parable of the Mustard Seed
3. Parable of the Strong Man
4. Parable of the New/Old Wineskins
5. Parable of the Tenants
6. Parable of the Fig Tree
7. Parable of the Faithful Servant

2 Miracles of Jesus Mentioned in All 4 Gospels

1. Feeding of the 5,000
2. The Resurrection

11 Miracles of Jesus Mentioned in 3 of the 4 Gospels

1. Healing Peter's mother-in-law
2. Healing the leper
3. Healing of the paralytic
4. Healing of the man with the withered hand
5. Calming the sea
6. Healing the demoniac
7. Healing the bleeding woman
8. Raising Jairus' daughter
9. Walking on water
10. Healing the demon-possessed boy
11. Healing the blind man

5 Miracles of Jesus Surprisingly Mentioned in Only 1 Gospel

1. Turning water into wine
2. Miraculous catch of fish
3. Raising the widow's son at Nain
4. Cleansing of the 10 lepers
5. Raising Lazarus from the dead

Top 10 Things You Need to Know About Moses

1. He was a Levite, meaning he came from the family line of Levi, one of the 12 sons of Jacob.
2. His older brother was Aaron.
3. His older sister was Miriam.
4. Moses got his name from Pharaoh's daughter, who found him floating in a basket on the Nile.
5. His name means "to draw from the water."
6. Moses spent 40 years living in Pharaoh's house. Forty years living in the wilderness. Forty years leading the Israelites to the border of the Promised Land.
7. Moses married Zipporah as a gift from her father, Jethro, since Moses rescued his daughters from an attack while they were at a well.
8. Moses had two sons: Gershom and Eliezer.
9. Moses died at the border of the Promised Land on Mount Nebo.
10. God buried Moses in a secret place.

11 Medical Conditions Jesus Healed

1. Severe pain
2. Demon possession
3. Seizures
4. Paralysis
5. Leprosy
6. Fever
7. Blindness
8. Mute
9. Lame (can't walk)
10. Deafness
11. Death

Top 5 Reasons Jesus Was Born in Bethlehem

1. David was born there, and God promised him that a king would come from David's line who would sit on the throne forever.
2. Micah 5:2 prophesied Bethlehem would be the Messiah's birthplace.
3. It's a small, humble city, which is the way Jesus lived.
4. The name of the city means "house of bread." Jesus said He was the "bread of life."
5. Bethlehem had lots of shepherds who raised sheep used as sacrifices in nearby Jerusalem. Jesus became the ultimate sacrifice, the Lamb of God who took away the sin of the world.

Top 10 Facts About the Wise Men

1. They were most likely from Persian descent, coming from the region of Iran, which is one thousand miles from Israel. They were all from one descent, not three different.

2. Wise men are mentioned in Daniel. Daniel saved the wise men when he correctly interpreted King Nebuchadnezzar's dream. They liked him.

3. Many believe the Scriptures were compiled during the Israelite exile to Babylon and Persia. That's where the wise men would have gotten the Scriptures for the prophecy about the star.

4. The wise men most likely read Numbers 24:17 talking about a star and a king.

5. Despite tradition, nobody knows the names of the wise men.

6. There were probably more than three wise men. We don't know the number, only that they brought three gifts.

7. They are also known as magi or kings.

8. Magi followed stars in the sky in a practice called astrology. They probably followed black magic.

9. They were not kings in the traditional sense (thrones and scepters), but the term means they were probably rich, smart, and highly respected.

10. Whatever they believed and whoever they were, by the time they saw the Christ child, they fell on their knees and worshiped Jesus!

3 Times Jesus Spoke Aramaic, and the Gospels Give the Meaning

1. Mark 5:41—"He took her by the hand and said to her, *'Talitha koum!'* (which means 'Little girl, I say to you, get up!')."
2. Mark 7:34—"He looked up to heaven and with a deep sigh said to him, *'Ephphatha!'* (which means 'Be opened!')."
3. Matthew 27:46—"About three in the afternoon Jesus cried out in a loud voice, *'Eli, Eli, lema sabachthani'* (which means 'My God, my God, why have you forsaken me?')."

6 Men the Bible Calls Handsome

1. Joseph
2. Saul
3. David
4. Absalom (David's son)
5. Adonijah (also David's son)
6. Daniel

3 People Who Angels Told Their Parents Their Names Before They Were Born

1. Ishmael
2. Jesus
3. John the Baptist

Top 10 Coolest Things About the Feeding of the 5,000

1. It's the only miracle besides the resurrection mentioned in all four Gospels.
2. It had a sequel—the feeding of the 4,000.
3. The Bible said Jesus fed 5,000 men, which means with women and children present, it could have been 15,000 people.
4. It occurred near Bethsaida, a fishing village, and it was the hometown of Philip, Andrew, and Peter.
5. Jesus multiplied fish—cooked and ready to eat. For fishermen in a fishing village that would be pretty impressive!
6. Jesus multiplied bread—baked and ready to eat.
7. Jesus started from five loaves and two fish to create this enormous buffet.
8. Everyone ate and was satisfied.
9. There were 12 basketfuls left over. Twelve is the number of the tribes of Israel. Jesus was saying He had come to feed the Jews. (For the feeding of the 4,000, Jesus fed Gentiles or Non-Jews. He came for them, too.)
10. Jesus had everyone sit in groups of 50 to 100, like small churches or small groups where they probably talked and shared about their feelings in seeing this miracle.

7 Things Jesus Said From the Cross

1. "*Eli, Eli, lema sabachthani?*' (which means, 'My God, my God, why have you forsaken me?')" (Matthew 27:46).
2. "Father, forgive them, for they do not know what they are doing" (Luke 23:34).
3. "Truly I tell you, today you will be with me in paradise" (Luke 23:43).

4. "Father, into your hands I commit my spirit" (Luke 23:46).
5. "'Woman, here is your son,' and to the disciple, 'Here is your mother'" (John 19:26–27).
6. "I am thirsty" (John 19:28).
7. "It is finished" (John 19:30).

7 Mean Things Jesus Called the Pharisees (and They Deserved It)

1. Hypocrites
2. Blind guides
3. Blind fools
4. Blind men
5. Whitewashed tombs
6. Snakes
7. Brood of vipers

3 Things Animals Said in the Bible

1. Balaam's donkey: "What have I done to you to make you beat me these three times?" (Numbers 22:28)
2. Balaam's donkey: "Am I not your own donkey, which you have always ridden, to this day? Have I been in the habit of doing this to you?" (Numbers 22:30)
3. An eagle in Revelation: "Woe! Woe! Woe to the inhabitants of the earth, because of the trumpet blasts about to be sounded by the other three angels!" (Revelation 8:13)

6 Names of Really Tall Tribes in the Bible

1. Emites
2. Anakites
3. Rephaites
4. Zamzummites
5. Gittites
6. Sabeans

4 Similarities Between Joseph, Son of Jacob (From Genesis), and Joseph, Jesus' Earthly Father

1. Both were descendants of Jacob.
2. Both had dreams.
3. Both were used by God to bring salvation to the world.
4. Both went to Egypt.

10 Similarities Between the Feeding of the 5,000 and the Feeding of the 4,000

1. Jesus made them both happen.
2. He had compassion on them before feeding them.
3. Both happened near the Sea of Galilee.
4. He healed people both times.
5. The menu for both was bread and fish.
6. Both times the disciples didn't know how to feed them.
7. Jesus gave thanks before both feedings.
8. Both times there were leftovers.
9. Both feedings fully satisfied those who were fed.
10. The gospels of Matthew and Mark tell both stories.

4 Reasons to Exempt Someone From Battle (According to Deuteronomy 20)

1. They just built a new house.
2. They just planted a new vineyard.
3. They just got married (or engaged).
4. They were afraid.

6 False Gods the One True God Really Hated

1. Molek/Molech
2. Ashtoreth
3. Asherah
4. Chemosh
5. Baal
6. Dagon

10 Impressive Old Testament Prophecies That Came True as Quoted by Matthew

1. Jesus would be born of a virgin. (Matthew 1:23, quoting Isaiah 7:14)
2. Jesus would be born in Bethlehem. (Matthew 2:6, quoting Micah 5:2)
3. Jesus would go to Egypt. (Matthew 2:15, quoting Hosea 11:1)
4. John the Baptist would prepare the people for Jesus. (Matthew 3:3, quoting Isaiah 40:3 and Matthew 11:10, quoting Malachi 3:1)
5. Jesus would live in Galilee. (Matthew 4:15, quoting Isaiah 9:1)
6. Jesus would heal diseases. (Matthew 8:17, quoting Isaiah 53:5)

7. Jesus would teach with parables. (Matthew 13:13–15, 35, quoting Psalm 78:2 and Isaiah 6:9–10)
8. Jesus would ride on a donkey and colt. (Matthew 21:4–5, quoting Zechariah 9:9)
9. When Jesus was arrested, His friends and disciples would scatter. (Matthew 26:31, quoting Zechariah 13:7)
10. Judas would betray Jesus for thirty pieces of silver, and that money would buy a potter's field. (Matthew 27:7–10, quoting Zechariah 11:12–13)

4 People in the Bible You Probably Didn't Think Were Related

1. Abraham and Sarah were half-brother and sister. (Genesis 20:12)
2. Mordecai and Esther were cousins. (Esther 2:7)
3. Mark and Barnabas were cousins. (Colossians 4:10)
4. Jesus and John the Baptist were related. (Luke 1:36)

9 Interesting Facts About the Temptation of Jesus

1. It happened right after Jesus' baptism when God spoke from heaven. This certainly caused many to be curious about Jesus . . . because He disappeared for 40 days.
2. The temptations happened for 40 days, the same number of days it rained for Noah and the number of days Moses spent on the mountain. Moses fasted, too, for 40 days.
3. The Gospel accounts said that Jesus did not eat food, but it says nothing about Him not drinking water. Moses didn't drink water on Mount Sinai. (Exodus 34:28)
4. Mark mentions that Jesus was with wild animals during that time.

5. Matthew and Mark mention that the angels ministered to Him.

6. Every time Jesus was tempted He responded with Scripture—and each time He quoted the book of Deuteronomy.

7. The temptations were all attempts by the devil to make Jesus do what the devil wanted Him to do. Turning stones to bread is not a sin. But following the devil's orders is a sin. The temptations were all about a power struggle. Who is really in charge? Jesus defeated Satan by saying "Don't put me to the test!"

8. Because the temptation occurred when Jesus was physically at His weakest, Satan never tried to tempt Jesus when He was well-fed and surrounded by friends. Since Jesus didn't cave in once, there's no way He could be tempted later.

9. The gospel of John does not mention the temptation.

5 Words Surprisingly Not Found in the Bible

1. Bible
2. Trinity
3. Rapture
4. Easter
5. Christmas

3 Greatest Miracles Joshua Witnessed in the book of Joshua

1. The parting of the Jordan River with the Israelites (Joshua 4)
2. The walls of Jericho falling down (Joshua 6)
3. The sun stopping for an entire day during battle (Joshua 10)

4 Names of Jesus' Brothers
(and He Had Sisters, Too, But They Aren't Named)

1. James
2. Joseph
3. Judas
4. Simon

7 Things Jesus Did on the Sabbath
That Angered the Pharisees

1. Allowed the disciples to pick grain in the field
2. Healed a man with a shriveled hand
3. Read from Isaiah saying He fulfilled the Scriptures
4. Healed a crippled woman
5. Healed a man with abnormal swelling
6. Healed a crippled man carrying a mat
7. Healed a blind man

3 Times Birthdays Were Celebrated in the Bible

1. Pharaoh (Genesis 40:20, during the time of Joseph)
2. Job's children (Job 1:4)
3. King Herod (Matthew 14:6)

5 People Who Encountered Magicians in the Bible

1. Joseph in Genesis 41, but the magicians could not interpret Pharaoh's dream.
2. Moses in Exodus 7–8 when they performed tricks that were just like the plagues but were eventually stumped and gave up.
3. Daniel in Daniel 2, when the magicians could not interpret the king's dream.
4. Peter and John in Acts 8 encountered a sorcerer (a type of magician who used tricks to fool people for money) named Simon.
5. Paul in Acts 13 met a sorcerer named Elymas and caused him to be blind.

27 People Who Saw Angels

1. Abraham
2. Hagar
3. Lot
4. Jacob
5. Moses
6. Balaam
7. Joshua
8. Gideon
9. Samson's parents
10. David
11. Elijah
12. Isaiah
13. Nebuchadnezzar when he saw the figure in the fire
14. Daniel

15. Zechariah (the prophet)
16. Mary
17. Joseph (Jesus' earthly father)
18. Jesus
19. Zechariah (John the Baptist's father)
20. Shepherds
21. Mary Magdalene
22. The apostles as a group when released from jail
23. Philip
24. Cornelius
25. Peter
26. Paul
27. John

10 Countries Mentioned in the Bible That Are Still Around Today

1. Egypt
2. Ethiopia
3. Greece
4. India
5. Israel
6. Italy
7. Lebanon
8. Malta
9. Spain
10. Syria

514 People Who Saw the Resurrected Jesus

1. Mary Magdalene
2. Peter
3. Thomas
4. Nathanael
5. James
6. John
7. 6 other apostles
8. Cleopas
9. Cleopas' companion on the road to Emmaus
10. 500 others as indicated by Paul in 1 Corinthians 15

WORDS in a WORD
FROM the WORD

//

NEW TESTAMENT

How many words can you make from the following words found in the Word?

PAUL—We found 3 possible words. Can you find more?

_____   _____   _____

SHEEP—We found 3 possible words. Can you find more?

_____   _____   _____

PETER—We found 4 possible words. Can you find more?

_____   _____   _____

_____

MARY—We found 8 possible words. Can you find more?

_____   _____   _____

_____   _____   _____

_____   _____

PARABLE—We found 12 possible words. Can you find more?

_____   _____   _____

_____   _____   _____

_____   _____   _____

_____   _____   _____

GALILEE—We found 15 possible words. Can you find more?

_____   _____   _____

_____   _____   _____

_____   _____   _____

_____   _____   _____

_____   _____   _____

BETHLEHEM—We found 24 possible words. Can you find more?

_____   _____   _____

_____   _____   _____

_____   _____   _____

_____   _____   _____

_____   _____   _____

_____   _____   _____

_____   _____   _____

_____   _____   _____

NAZARETH—We found 43 possible words. Can you find more?

_____   _____   _____

_____   _____   _____

_____   _____   _____

_____   _____   _____

_____   _____   _____

_____   _____   _____

_____   _____   _____

_____   _____   _____

_____   _____   _____

_____   _____   _____

_____   _____   _____

_____   _____   _____

_____

CAN'T PRAY IF YOU DON'T KNOW the WORDS

Fill in the blanks with the right words to complete Jesus' prayer in Matthew 6:9–13.

Forgive	Heaven	Debtors	Today
Kingdom	Deliver	Father	Will
Bread	Earth	Temptation	Name

Our _____ in _____,

hallowed be your _____,

your _____ come,

your _____ be done,

on _____ as it is in heaven.

Give us _____ our daily _____

And _____ us our debts,

as we also have forgiven our _____.

And lead us not into _____,

but _____ us from the evil one.

Answer:

Our **Father** in **heaven**,
hallowed be your **name**,
your **kingdom** come,
your **will** be done,
on **earth** as it is in heaven.
Give us **today** our daily **bread**.
And **forgive** us our debts,
as we also have forgiven our **debtors**.
And lead us not into **temptation**,
but **deliver** us from the evil one.

ARE YOU SMARTER
THAN KiNG SOLOMON?

New Testament

According to Jesus, what three things below don't stress out about life, so He encourages us to also not worry?

A. Squirrels

B. Birds

C. Grass

D. Weeds

E. Bananas

F. Lilies

Answer: B, C, and F

How many times did the rooster crow, indicating Peter's denial of Jesus?

A. One time

B. Two times

C. Three times

D. The rooster didn't crow, it laughed.

Answer: B. The rooster crowed two times. Peter denied three times.

According to Jesus, what three things cannot ruin or steal our treasure if we keep it in heaven?

A. Vermin (rats)

B. Erosion

C. Ants

D. Robots

E. Thieves

F. Moths

Answer: A, E, and F

At the Last Supper, which three items did Jesus tell His followers they must go and get?

A. Purse

B. Bag

C. Sword

D. Sandals

Answer: A, B, and C

James, in chapter 3, doesn't have a lot of nice things to say about the tongue. Which of these things did James compare the tongue to? (4 answers)

A. Deadly poison

B. Forest fire

C. Ship's rudder

D. Loose cannon

E. Untamed animal

F. Pointy arrow

Answers: A, B, C, and E

Which of these tasty foods did Jesus talk about? (4 answers)

A. Mustard seeds

B. Oranges

C. Grapes

D. Bread

E. Lamb chops

F. Broiled fish

Answers: A, C, D, and F

Jesus told Peter to go catch a fish where he would find something in its mouth. What was it?

A. A worm

B. A clue

C. Another fish

D. A coin

Answer: D. When the temple officials asked about Jesus paying a tax, Jesus said the money would be found in a fish's mouth. You've heard of a piggy bank? This is a fishy bank.

When Jesus rode into Jerusalem a week before His death, what did He ride on?

A. The backs of his apostles

B. A white horse

C. A donkey and a colt

D. He crowd-surfed

Answer: C. The donkey and the colt fulfilled a prophecy in Zechariah 9:9. They were humble creatures just like Jesus was humble.

When Jesus died on the cross, what happened in Jerusalem?

A. An earthquake struck
B. Darkness came over the land
C. The temple curtain tore in two
D. Dead people stepped out of their graves

Answers: All four happened!

Which two of these foods did John the Baptist eat?

A. Locusts
B. Snakes
C. Chickens
D. Honey

Answers: A and D. It says he dined on locusts and honey. Locusts dipped in honey . . . mmmm, sweet and crunchy!

Who in the Bible thought they saw a ghost? (2 answers)

A. King Saul
B. Paul
C. The apostles
D. King David

Answers: A and C. King Saul saw the spirit of Samuel, and the apostles thought Jesus was a ghost walking on the water.

Which two Old Testament men appeared with Jesus when He transfigured on the mountain?

A. David

B. Moses

C. Adam

D. Elijah

Answers: B and D. When Jesus transfigured—or showed His heavenly self—to Peter, James, and John, Moses and Elijah appeared next to him. They say "three's a crowd," but what a crowd that was!

Which of these are actual people named Simon in the Bible? (5 answers)

A. Simon the Leper

B. Simon the Sez

C. Simon the Zealot

D. Simon the Sorcerer

E. Simon from Cyrene

F. Simon the Simple

G. Simon the Tanner

H. Simon the Cowell

Answers: A, C, D, E, and G

What does the name *Gethsemane*, where Jesus was arrested, mean?

A. Prayer garden

B. Olive press

C. Private property

D. Public park

Answer: B. It was a garden of olive trees, where the olives were picked and pressed into olive oil.

Who was the man that the crowd wanted released from prison instead of Jesus?

A. Barsabbas

B. Barnabas

C. Barney

D. Barabbas

Answer: D. Barabbas was arrested for insurrection and murder, yet the crowd felt he was a better person to be running around the streets rather than Jesus.

What does the name *Golgotha*, where Jesus was crucified, mean?

A. Place of the cross

B. Place of sadness

C. Place of the skull

D. Place you don't want to go alone at night

Answer: C

Which of these were the jobs Jesus' apostles had before He called them to follow Him? (2 answers)

A. Tax collector
B. Bread maker
C. Fisherman
D. Farmer

Answer: A and C. We only know that Matthew (aka Levi) was a tax collector and that Peter, Andrew, James, and John were fishermen. The occupations of the rest are unknown.

How much food did Jesus start with before He miraculously multiplied it for the 5,000?

A. 2 loaves and 5 fishes
B. 1 loaf and 1 fish
C. 5 loaves and 2 fishes
D. The number for Pizza Hut

Answer: C

Which of these were real Marys found in the New Testament? (4 answers)

A. Mary Magdalene
B. Mary sister of Martha
C. Mary Christmas
D. Mary mother of James and Joseph
E. Mary mother of Jesus
F. Mary who had a little lamb

Answers: A, B, D, and E. Popular name then and now!

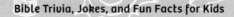

What was the bread made of that Jesus multiplied for the 5,000?

    A. Whole wheat

    B. Rye

    C. Sourdough

    D. Barley

Answer: D

10-4-10

The following 10 people are mentioned in Jesus' family tree. Put them in order of their birth from 1 to 10.

____ David

____ Judah

____ Joseph

____ Solomon

____ Jacob

____ Isaac

____ Boaz

____ Hezekiah

____ Abraham

____ Jesse

Answers: 1. Abraham 2. Isaac 3. Jacob 4. Judah 5. Boaz 6. Jesse 7. David 8. Solomon 9. Hezekiah 10. Joseph

SO YOU WANT
to BE an APOSTLE?

In the New Testament, being an apostle after Jesus left the earth was tough. The book of Acts tells of all the troubles they faced trying to get the Good News out to the world. Look at all the difficulties they battled and ask yourself, would you be willing to be an apostle?

- ▶ Put in jail
- ▶ Threatened
- ▶ Put on trial
- ▶ Whipped
- ▶ Hit with stones
- ▶ Chained
- ▶ Killed
- ▶ Involved in riots
- ▶ Endured hurricanes
- ▶ Shipwrecked
- ▶ Constantly in danger
- ▶ Hunger and thirst

BUT they also got to see . . .

- ▶ Many people accept Christ and be saved
- ▶ The Holy Spirit enter the lives of people

- ▸ Churches started
- ▸ Healing from physical problems (blindness, can't walk)
- ▸ Healing from sickness and diseases
- ▸ People raised from the dead
- ▸ All kinds of other amazing miracles!

The good outweighs the bad. . . .

SEEK and YOU WiLL FiND

Parable Or Not

Which of the following parables did Jesus talk about, and which are made up? Cross out the ones that don't belong.

Parable of the Wise and Foolish Builder

Parable of the Sower

Parable of the Rich Beggar

Parable of the Lovely Leper

Parable of the Weeds

Parable of the Mustard Seed

Parable of the Hidden Treasure

Parable of the Net

Parable of the Angry Goat

Parable of the Unmerciful Servant

Parable of the Tangled Vine

Parable of the Vineyard Workers

Parable of the Dumb Disciple

Parable of the Tenants

Parable of the Wedding Banquet

Parable of the Sheep and Goats

Parable of the Lost Pigs

Parable of the Lost Sheep

Parable of the Good Samaritan

Parable of the Shrewd Manager

Parable of the Persistent Widow

Parable of the Flying Fish

Parable of the Ten Minas

Parable of the Blushing Bride

True Parables:
Wise and Foolish Builder, Sower, Weeds, Mustard Seed, Hidden Treasure, Net, Unmerciful Servant, Vineyard Workers, Tenants, Wedding Banquet, Sheep and Goats, Lost Sheep, Good Samaritan, Shrewd Manager, Persistent Widow, Ten Minas

Pack Lightly

When Jesus sent His disciples out into the world, He told them not to take a lot of stuff but to rely on God to provide. Circle the things Jesus specifically told His disciples NOT to take with them on their journey.

Staff	Sudoku
Rope	Sandals
Bread	Yarmulke
Bag	Gold
Suitcase	Sunscreen
Bible	Bronze
iPad	Silver
Money	Copper
Extra shirt	Tools
Extra pants	Passport

Answers: staff, bread, bag, money, extra shirt, sandals, gold, bronze, silver, copper

Are You Gifted?

When somebody receives Jesus Christ, the Holy Spirit comes to live inside them. The Holy Spirit equips that person with a spiritual gift that helps them encourage the body of Christ. Circle the spiritual gifts mentioned by Paul in 1 Corinthians 12.

Humor	Athleticism
Serving	Miraculous powers
Wisdom	Prophecy
Speaking well	Disagreement
Knowledge	Discernment
Singing	Happiness
Acting	Speaking in tongues
Faith	Interpretation of tongues
Healing	Curling of tongues

Answers: serving, wisdom, knowledge, faith, healing, miraculous powers, prophecy, discernment, speaking in tongues, interpretation of tongues

Act Like a Fruit!

In Galatians, Paul talks about the fruits of the Spirit—how a believer acts when the Holy Spirit lives in his or her heart. Circle the fruits of the Spirit from the list below, then write them in the order Paul mentions them in Galatians 5:22–23 (HCSB).

Patience   Gentleness

Intelligence   Love

Self-Control   Faith

Encouragement   Organization

Wisdom   Peace

Politeness   Quietness

Kindness   Hospitality

Joy   Goodness

Quickness   Enthusiasm

_____   _____   _____

_____   _____   _____

_____   _____   _____

Answers: Love, joy, peace, patience, kindness, goodness, faith, gentleness, self-control

Very Revealing Cities

Which of these cities are mentioned in the book of Revelation? (7 answers)

Pergamum   Nazareth

Jericho   Philadelphia

Bethlehem   Galatia

Ephesus   Rome

Laodicea   Thyatira

Corinth   Smyrna

Sardis   Gomorrah

Answers: Pergamum, Ephesus, Laodicea, Sardis, Philadelphia, Thyatira, Smyrna

I AM . . .

Which of these "I AM" statements did Jesus really say? (7 answers)

I am the way, the truth, and the life.

I am the one and only.

I am the Good Shepherd.

I am the bread of life.

I am the doctor.

I am the resurrection and the life.

I am the rock.

I am your neighbor.

I am the light of the world.

I am the gate.

I am the vine.

I am a little lamb.

Answers:
I am the way, the truth, and the life.
I am the Good Shepherd.
I am the bread of life.
I am the resurrection and the life.
I am the light of the world.
I am the gate.
I am the vine.

WHAT in the WORD?

Do we know what Jesus looked like?

No gospel mentions anything about Jesus' looks. We can only assume that He looked like other Jews at that time. Only one passage in the Old Testament hints at His looks, and it was written 700 years before He walked the earth.

> He grew up before him like a tender shoot,
>   and like a root out of dry ground.
> He had no beauty or majesty to attract us to him,
>   nothing in his appearance that we should desire him.
> He was despised and rejected by mankind,
>   a man of suffering, and familiar with pain.
> Like one from whom people hide their faces
>   he was despised, and we held him in low esteem.
>
> Isaiah 53:2–3

This passage says Jesus did not attract people by His looks. He was a regular-looking guy—not a hunky model or a tall, dark, and handsome carpenter. Isaiah also prophesied that Jesus would live a hard life (and maybe it showed), but that He had an extraordinary love inside Him that drew many to Him. His attractiveness was His love.

Who were the apostles?

An apostle was one called by God to spread the Good News. Here were the men who were called apostles in the New Testament (and the other names they were known by).

1. Peter / Simon Peter
2. Andrew
3. Bartholomew / Nathanael
4. James, the Elder
5. James, the Lesser / Younger
6. John
7. Judas—betrayed Jesus and died
8. Jude / Thaddeus
9. Matthew / Levi
10. Philip
11. Simon the Zealot
12. Thomas / Didymus
13. Matthias—When Judas betrayed Jesus, Matthias was elected to fill his place.
14. Paul/Saul—In Romans 1:1, Paul called himself an apostle. He was a last-minute addition but because Jesus called him directly from heaven, he's considered an apostle.

What's the difference between an apostle and a disciple?

An *apostle* was called to follow Jesus Christ. Jesus asked Paul, Andrew, Nathanael, and others to follow Him.

Disciples followed Jesus after hearing His words and message.

It's the difference between being called to follow and deciding you want to follow. You can be a disciple, but you can't choose to be an apostle. You must be called to that.

TALK the TALK

Here are some fun questions to talk to your parents and friends about. Use them while you're driving in the car or sitting around the dinner table.

What part of God's **creation** do you love the most?

What would be the hardest part about being on **Noah's ark** for so long?

In Genesis, **Joseph** had 11 brothers and one sister. Would you like a family that big? More brothers or more sisters?

Joseph's dad gave him a colorful coat that made his brothers **jealous**. What gift could your parents give your brothers or sisters that might make you jealous?

Which of the Egyptian **plagues**—frogs, gnats, flies, hail, or darkness—would you hate the most and why?

How would you feel having to kill an **animal** for your sins?

If you met a talking **donkey**, like Balaam did, what would you ask him?

What other animal would you like to **talk** to?

If you were Samson, when would you like to use your **strength**?

How would you feel if you lived in **Jericho** and an army marched around the city for seven days?

Have you ever stood up to a **bully** like David did?

David and Jonathan were close **friends**. Who is your best friend? Why?

God told King Solomon he could have whatever he wanted. Solomon asked for **wisdom**. What would you ask God for?

God sometimes changed people's **names**. If you could change your name, what would it be?

The youngest **king** of Judah was eight years old. Would you want to be a king at that age? Would you be a good king? What's the first rule you would impose?

How would you react if all those bad things happened to you like it did with **Job**? Would you think God was mad at you?

What would you do if God **spoke** directly to you like He did with Moses and Job?

Proverbs points out a lot of **foolish** behavior. What things do you consider foolish that your friends do?

What things do you consider **wise**?

What kind of animal do you think is wise or that you can **learn** from?

If you were given 15 more years to live like **Hezekiah**, what would you do with that time?

How cool would it be to spend a night with **lions** like Daniel did (assuming they didn't want to eat you)? What would you do in that den with friendly lions?

What would it be like to be in the belly of a great **fish** for three days?

If God called you to go somewhere like He did **Jonah**, would you run away? Especially if that place was dangerous?

Do you want God to give you a **message**—like a prophet—even though that message might be unpopular with people?

What is your greatest **treasure**?

What do you think it was like growing up with **Jesus**?

What would the dinner table conversations be like if Jesus was your **brother**?

Why do you think Jesus grew up in a **carpenter's house**?

If Jesus walked up to you and asked you to **follow** Him, would you drop everything and go?

Which of Jesus' **miracles** do you wish you were there to see? (His baptism, feeding 5,000, walking on water, raising Lazarus from the dead, the Resurrection . . .)

Why do you think the man's friends lowered him through the **roof** to be with Jesus? Do you want friends like that? How did the man whose roof was destroyed feel?

If Jesus **came back** to earth while you were alive, what do you want to be doing at the time?

What do you think the **food** is like in heaven?

Who is the first person you want to see in **heaven**?

Why do you think we **pray** if God already knows the answer?

If God could **promise** you one thing, what would you want it to be?

Hebrews 13:2 says there are times we could be entertaining strangers that could be **angels**. Does that scare you or encourage you?

Do you wish the **Bible** were longer or shorter?

At the end of the **gospel** of John, it says there were many other stories about Jesus that the author couldn't tell because he didn't have room. Do you hope to hear them someday?

Paul talked many times about **spiritual gifts** God gives us to help the church. What role in the church do you want to do someday?

Jesus fed the **5,000** with bread and fish. If Jesus miraculously fed your school, what food would He choose?

Do you think you would have denied knowing **Christ** like Peter did? Have you ever denied Jesus with your friends?

If you were alive on that **Easter Sunday**, the morning Jesus rose from the dead, where would you be?

ARE YOU on the ROAD to HEAVEN?

The book of Romans has some of the best verses to understand what a relationship with Jesus Christ is all about so that you can be with God forever in heaven.

> . . . all have sinned and fall short of the glory of God. . . .
>
> Romans 3:23

We are all sinners, and in God's eyes we must be separated from Him because He is perfect and we are not.

> For the wages of sin is death, but the gift of God is eternal life in Christ Jesus our Lord.
>
> Romans 6:23

The penalty of sin is death. Death is separation from this earth and separation from God. We cannot be in God's presence ever because of our sin.

> But God demonstrates his own love for us in this: While we were still sinners, Christ died for us.
>
> Romans 5:8

Since the penalty of sin is death, someone needs to die for our sins. If not us, then who? God loved us and sent His son Jesus Christ to die for us. Jesus paid the penalty by dying on the cross.

Therefore, there is now no condemnation for those who are in Christ Jesus. . . .

Romans 8:1

If you are in a relationship with Jesus Christ (loving Him and trusting Him), then God does not hold any penalty against you. He sees you as He sees His Son.

If you declare with your mouth, "Jesus is Lord," and believe in your heart that God raised him from the dead, you will be saved.

Romans 10:9

If you can say Jesus is Lord and believe that God raised Jesus from the dead, you are saved from eternal death and separation from God. You are now His son/daughter.

Is that you? Have you done this? Simply pray:

Lord, forgive me for my sins. I accept Jesus and love Him because He died for me on the cross. He has taken away the penalty of my sin. I believe He is your Son, sent to this earth to live and die, and then rise again, conquering sin and death. He is Lord of this earth, and I allow Him to be Lord of my life.

Try your hand at creating your own knock-knock jokes with people from the Bible. Say the names out loud and listen to what they sound like. For instance, "Moses" sounds like "Mo says." Mark is already a word in itself. So the answer to the knock-knock joke would be "Mo says . . ." or "Mark my words . . ." Here are some other names to play with: Cain, Abel, Eli, Lot, Pharoah, Caesar, Pilate. Read through your Bible to find more!

Think of Bible puns and put them into question-and-answer jokes. Here's a typical pattern to get you thinking: Why did God send frogs to Egypt? Because He was hop-ping mad!

Read through your Bible and look for unusual facts. Then write them down as questions and stump your friends!

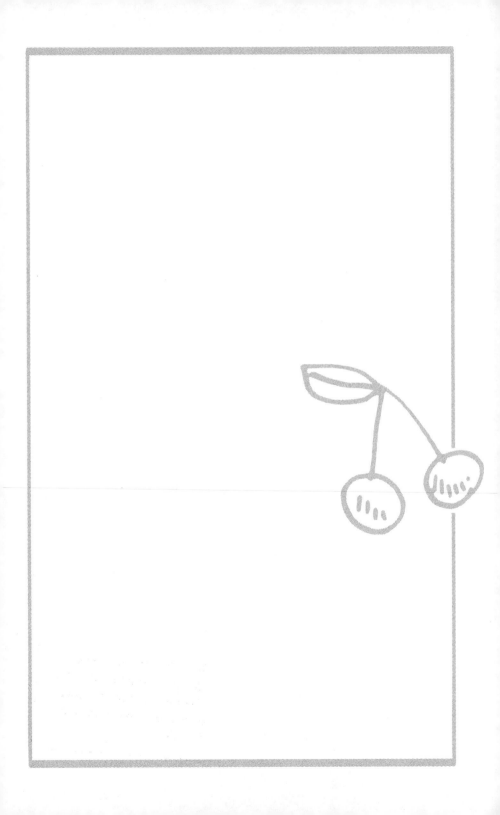

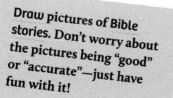
Draw pictures of Bible stories. Don't worry about the pictures being "good" or "accurate"—just have fun with it!

TROY SCHMIDT is an author and television writer with credits at Disney, Nickelodeon, Tommy Nelson, and Lifeway. He has written for Max Lucado's HERMIE AND FRIENDS series and was the consulting producer for *The American Bible Challenge* with Jeff Foxworthy. His other book titles include *Saved, Release, 40 Days, Chapter by Chapter, In His Shoes: The Life of Jesus,* and many others. Troy has also written several children's books, including *Little Tree Found* and *Their Side of the Story.* He is a campus pastor at First Baptist Church of Windermere, Florida. Troy and his wife have three grown sons and make their home in Florida.